GROSS
DECEPTION

GROSS DECEPTION

A Tale of Shifting Markets, Shrinking Margins & the New Truth of Used Car Profitability

DALE POLLAK

vAuto Press

Published by vAuto Press
Oakbrook Terrace, IL
www.vauto.com

Distributed by Greenleaf Book Group

For ordering information or special discounts for bulk purchases, please contact Greenleaf Book Group at PO Box 91869, Austin, TX 78709, 512.891.6100.

Design and composition by Greenleaf Book Group
Cover design by The Mx Group, www.themxgroup.com

Publisher's Cataloging-in-Publication data is available.

Print ISBN: 978-0-9992427-3-5

eBook ISBN: 978-0-9992427-4-2

Audiobook ISBN: 978-0-9992427-5-9

Part of the Tree Neutral® program, which offsets the number of trees consumed in the production and printing of this book by taking proactive steps, such as planting trees in direct proportion to the number of trees used: www.treeneutral.com

Printed in the United States of America on acid-free paper

20 21 22 23 24 25   11 10 9 8 7 6 5 4 3 2

First Edition

CONTENTS

ACKNOWLEDGMENTS   ix

PREFACE:
Gross Deception and the New Truth of Used
Vehicle Profitability   xi

INTRODUCTION:
A Second, Profit-Powered Wind for Dealers in
Used Vehicles   1

CHAPTER 1:
Margin Compression Leaves a Mark   9

CHAPTER 2:
A Stretch of Serious Soul-Searching   15

CHAPTER 3:
A Revelation: A Troubling Cost to Market Problem   21

CHAPTER 4:
The New Math of the Used Car Business   31

CHAPTER 5:
Balancing the New Math Equation   35

CHAPTER 6:

Pushback on the Balanced New Math Equation   45

CHAPTER 7:

Balancing the New Math Equation: From Hockey
to Figure Skating   51

CHAPTER 8:

A Question of Time and Money in Used Cars   59

CHAPTER 9:

A Hole in the Used Car Universe   69

CHAPTER 10:

Strange Bedfellows: Bananas and Used Vehicles   75

CHAPTER 11:

A New Algorithm and a Holy S**t Moment   81

CHAPTER 12:

A Composite of Investment Distress and Indifference   89

CHAPTER 13:

Who's Going to Jump on the Grenade?   97

CHAPTER 14:

A Trifecta of Insights to Make
Investment-Smart Acquisitions   103

CHAPTER 15:

The Makings of the ProfitTime Moniker   117

CHAPTER 16:

Understanding the "Why" behind ProfitTime   121

CHAPTER 17:

ProfitTime in Practice—Fixing Your Inventory
Investment Inversion   133

CHAPTER 18:

Parameters of Proper ProfitTime Pricing   143

CHAPTER 19:

Attuning Your ProfitTime Pricing Strategy to
Your Market   153

CHAPTER 20:

A Quick Point on Platinum Vehicle Pushback   161

CHAPTER 21:

Using ProfitTime to Make More
Investment-Minded Acquisitions   165

CHAPTER 22:

ProfitTime's Change Management Opportunity   173

EPILOGUE:

A Broader View of ProfitTime
in Progress—and a Promise   181

ABOUT THE AUTHOR   191

ACKNOWLEDGMENTS

While writing a book is, in many ways, a solitary affair, I am blessed to have had a lot of help.

There's my wife, Nancy, my three sons, and the rest of my family. You gave me the space I needed over the past two years to reflect, ruminate, and work my way through the troubling trends that have emerged in the used vehicle business.

Without your grace, love, and understanding, I might still be on the fishing dock, and this book would never have arrived.

The same is true with my colleagues at Cox Automotive and vAuto—specifically Alex Taylor, CEO of Cox Enterprises; Sandy Schwartz, president of Cox Automotive; Keith Jezek, president of Cox Automotive's Retail Solutions Group; Randy Kobat, senior vice president of vAuto; and my assistant, Susan Taft.

Without their blessing, patience, and trust, this book would still be rattling around in my brain rather than laid out in the following pages.

I owe a deep thanks to two other vAuto colleagues—Chris

Stutsman, senior director of product innovation, and Lance Helgeson, director of industry analysis.

Chris helped me turn some of my concerns and suspicions about the used car business into the cold, hard facts that define the new truth of used car profitability. His important work went even further. It led to a new inventory management methodology and metric that is proving to be a game-changer for dealers.

Meanwhile, Lance has turned my revelations, riffs, and ruffles into cogent, compelling copy. This is our fifth book together, and none would have been possible without Lance lending his thoughtful insights, perspective, and writing skills to each effort.

I must also share my sincere gratitude, respect, and thanks to the dealers who joined me on the book journey. You didn't have to take the time, share your perspectives, and entrust me with your stories.

But you did, and I thank you.

And finally, there's each of you. You didn't have to pick up or even open this book.

But you did, and I thank you.

PREFACE

GROSS DECEPTION AND THE NEW TRUTH OF USED VEHICLE PROFITABILITY

G ross is generally good in the used car business.

If they're making good gross, dealers believe they're making good money.

That's why, historically, dealers have tended to focus on front-end gross and, in more recent years, total gross as yardsticks to measure their used vehicle performance.

But this long-standing emphasis on gross profit has led to a kind of deception.

While dealers have been focusing on gross profit and volume as the primary drivers of their money-making efforts in used cars, they haven't been making as much money.

Many dealers are aware that front-end grosses certainly aren't what they used to be. Some have even come to accept low- or even no-gross deals as a new kind of normal given the pressures of a market where there's greater efficiency and pricing transparency for used vehicle buyers.

But I've come to understand that while dealers may believe they're at least making *some* money when they earn gross profit, that's not always the case.

In fact, I believe we've arrived at a time when making gross profit is no longer a guarantee that your used vehicle department will produce a positive net profit when you wrap up a month and account for all the expenses associated with selling your used cars.

I've spent the past two years studying this situation, trying to find and understand what dealers may be missing or overlooking as they retail ever-higher numbers of used vehicles and see ever-smaller net profitability for all their hard work.

The problem, I've found, rests with the long-standing belief in the power of gross profit itself, and the ways dealers generally manage and measure the gross profit potential of every used vehicle.

My work has revealed that associating a vehicle's days in inventory with its profit potential, in today's margin-compressed market, is a gross deception.

I've found that believing you can make up for ever-smaller front-end gross profits by selling more used vehicles to produce total gross profit is a gross deception.

I've determined that simply speeding up your sales velocity to maximize gross profit is yet another gross deception—one that, surprisingly, can make a dealer's net profit disappear more quickly than it might otherwise.

I've realized that it's my calling, duty, and mission to help dealers get out of the gross deception rut.

I've learned a lot in the past two years—specific insights about the used car business that suggest that much of what we believe to be true about used car profitability isn't true any longer.

This book presents the elements of what I am calling the New Truth of Used Vehicle Profitability, which I believe can help dealers regain, if not restore, some of the net profits in used vehicles that have fallen fast in recent years.

The book showcases how dealers are accepting the new truth and adopting a different way of managing their used vehicle business—a management method that centers every used vehicle decision on each vehicle's inherent net profit or return on investment (ROI) potential, rather than the gross profit dealers might believe a vehicle can make.

The new truth represents a new world order where gross profit and total gross still matter, but they take a back seat to the higher priority of ensuring your used vehicle department earns the net profit and ROI it deserves every time you choose to acquire and retail a car.

It's time for dealers to leave the gross deceptions behind and get on with making the used vehicle business fun and profitable again.

INTRODUCTION

A SECOND, PROFIT-POWERED WIND FOR DEALERS IN USED VEHICLES

I t was roughly 15 years ago when I set out with a day-for-hire driver to sell the first iteration of vAuto to dealers.

My driver, Jim, couldn't hear too well. He might have been as legally deaf as I'm legally blind.

But his price was right, and I needed a way to get around the Chicago area to pitch the idea that, thanks to the rise of the Internet, dealers needed to shed the traditional used vehicle management practices they'd employed for the better part of 100 years.

It was rough going, right from the start.

It was probably our third day, when Jim and I encountered what might charitably be described as stiff resistance.

Not long after the introductions, the dealer stopped me. He asked if he was on the TV show *Candid Camera*.

I asked him what he meant.

"I got a blind guy and a deaf guy here telling me how to sell used cars?"

That was the first time I got asked to leave a dealership while sharing the idea of Velocity Method of Management. It wasn't the last.

Flash forward two years.

I'd grown accustomed to the drumbeat of my daily routine. Get up. Catch a plane. Meet a dealer. Meet another dealer. Find a hotel. Set the room temperature at 69 degrees. Get some sleep. Do it again tomorrow.

By this time, I was on a first-name basis with some of the TSA and Southwest Airlines employees I encountered at Chicago's Midway Airport, sometimes two or three times a week. My travels also took me much farther away from home, which gave Jim more time to spend with his grandkids.

I felt like I was making some progress. The number of dealers who were interested in vAuto and signing up was growing.

The growth wasn't as fast as I would have liked and my creditors might have preferred, but my little company was moving forward. I was also becoming a fierce weekend napper, if the family schedule allowed, to make up for the rest I could never seem to find on the road.

I remember two things about this grind-it-out period:

First, I was gaining confidence that I was really onto something that might profoundly and significantly change the car business. The dealers who had begun using vAuto and following Velocity principles, who understood the Internet's then-nascent role in helping consumers shop for and price used vehicles, were making waves in their local markets.

They were selling cars. They had more customers in their showrooms. They had their cars online. They were paying attention not only to how many cars they sold and their front-end gross profits, but the efficiency and throughput of their used vehicle operations and the total gross it generated for their businesses.

The dealers were focused on how *fast* they sold their vehicles and how the used vehicle department drove a wheel of fortune across service, finance and insurance (F&I), and new vehicles.

The second thing I vividly recall is the pain many dealers felt as they transitioned to Velocity.

Many had to take a serious dose of medicine in the form of five- and six-figure losses that came with retailing, or wholesaling, 100-day-old and older inventory that they still believed, maybe one day, might deliver the gross profit they expected.

For a time, it seemed like adopting Velocity principles and finding success was a 50/50 proposition for dealers. Some made it work; others found it incredibly difficult and frustrating.

It was particularly difficult for dealers to stop applying a standard "cost-up" approach to pricing their used vehicles. This practice had become so entrenched and ingrained that it seemed anathema for dealers to do anything different.

I sometimes felt like a bug-eyed preacher, pounding the podium while making the case that prevailing market prices mattered more as a retail price reference point than what they paid for a vehicle.

It was also hard for dealers to let go of the belief that it was OK to let a vehicle age.

Despite the ever-smaller and ever-more-sparse showroom traffic logs they saw every Saturday, dealers had a hard time shedding the idea that "there's an ass for every seat" and a buyer would show up to pay their retail asking price.

It was around this time that vAuto implemented the concept of providing a Performance Manager for every vAuto client.

The struggles we saw at dealerships spawned a sense of responsibility for their success. I understood we had to do better than a 50/50 win rate with dealers. We knew it was on us to help dealers make the transition and see success.

I also couldn't afford to spend hours every weekend, like I'd been doing for months, on the phone with dealers, explaining the hows and whys of Velocity implementation.

My wife, Nancy, never once complained that I gave too much to my work and too little to my family.

But in my heart, I knew it was true.

By 2010, vAuto had gained critical mass in the market.

Despite all the early challenges and travails, and the hundreds of dealers who tried and quit the Velocity Method of Management at least once, the company I started in my kitchen had become a proven, reliable way for dealers to maximize the efficiency, performance, and profitability of their used vehicle department.

It was a heady time for me and everyone else on the vAuto team. We knew we were changing the industry for the better. We were providing a level of service and value that dealers were unaccustomed to seeing from their vendor partners.

I was proud, but I was also worried sick. Every day, I woke up with the fear that it could all go away. Dealers would lose their faith and trust, and I'd be out of business.

Over time, I came to recognize my fear as a bit genetic and irrational.

By this time, thousands of dealers had invested their confidence, faith, money, and trust in Velocity principles, vAuto, and me.

All of us at vAuto understood that our mission to change an industry and help dealers be more successful in used vehicles was becoming true. We were making a difference.

That year, I made the decision to sell vAuto to Cox Automotive. In order to continue making a difference with dealers, I believed it was necessary to become part of an organization that understood the entire ecosystem of automotive retailing and that shared my appreciation and respect for the dealers who paid the bills.

On the way home from signing the acquisition deal in Atlanta, I wasn't counting the money.

I was counting my blessings.

All the dealers who took a flier on me and vAuto and made it work, despite the pain.

All the forgiveness I received from my family for a dad who, despite trying hard, wasn't there as often as I could or should have been.

All the gratitude I felt for having found, or been given, a rare opportunity to change and disrupt an industry in a way that proved to be a win-win for all involved.

Today, I still feel the gratitude. In fact, it's the primary

motivator for me to press on with the mission of helping dealers become more efficient, profitable, and successful automotive retailers.

But I've arrived at another crossroads.

As I'll detail in this book, we've discovered a hole in the used
car universe that needs to be fixed.

It's a hole that's caused by our industry's collective reliance
on a gross deception—that using the calendar, or days in inventory, to measure and manage a used vehicle's return on investment (ROI) or net profit potential is the best way to make
money in used vehicles.

In fact, as we'll detail in upcoming chapters, this belief in managing gross is deeply flawed and damaging to net profitability.

We've discovered that the hole creates profound and costly
investment inefficiencies in used vehicle departments at nearly
every dealership.

It's a hole that the Velocity Method of Management may, in
some cases, make even worse.

It's a hole that will take a significant commitment, discipline,
and, yes, some financial pain for dealers to correct.

It's a hole I never imagined might exist or one that I might
discover.

But the good news is that dealers who endeavor to address
the hole have an unprecedented opportunity—a brisk second
wind, if you will, that will help them improve the performance
and profitability of their used vehicle operations at a time when
the market seems to be eating away at the net profits dealers
have long enjoyed when they retail used vehicles.

That's why I'm writing this book.

In the past year, I've been working intently with dealers who are adopting a new way to manage used vehicles based on their investment value and net profit potential.

It's a philosophy that asks dealers to embrace a fairly simple idea: To combat margin compression, you have to shift from thinking about how long you hold a used vehicle to the net profit potential, or investment value, each used vehicle holds.

This is a profound shift that is anything but easy to make.

The book is aimed at helping dealers successfully complete what can be a painful transition to a different way of doing business.

The book is about my journey to discover the new truths of used vehicle profitability, and the individual journeys dealers take as they accept and adopt them.

It's a journey that, like Velocity adoption, offers a deep sense of fulfillment, satisfaction, and financial rewards for dealers who successfully reach the destination.

But it's also a journey that isn't right for everyone, especially those who can't shake the grip of gross deception and refuse to accept the new truth of used vehicle profitability.

I appreciate your interest in the book, my journey, and the one you may choose to make.

Thank you. Enjoy the read.

CHAPTER 1

MARGIN COMPRESSION LEAVES A MARK

You'd be hard-pressed to find anyone who'd consider the period between 2011 and 2016 as anything but a go-go run for car dealers.

Franchised dealers who were fortunate enough to survive the Great Recession were being rewarded for their resilience and, in some cases, pure luck.

New vehicle sales rose every year between 2011 and 2016, including a three-year stretch where sales grew by more than one million vehicles each year.

We had a similar story in used vehicles.

Overall sales of used vehicles grew every year in this period except for 2013, when retail sales dipped a bit. The following year, however, overall volumes gained back the lost ground and then some.

It was almost as if those who had a dealership and wanted to sell more cars, could.

I distinctly remember the National Automobile Dealers Association (NADA) convention in early 2017 in New Orleans.

It was a party-like atmosphere. NADA and its dealer members were celebrating the group's 100th birthday, and we were gathered in the fun-friendly Big Easy.

As I wrote in my NADA blog posts from the convention, dealers were "buoyant" and downright "thirsty" for even more good times.

But I was in a different place.

I wasn't feeling the good times and the positive vibes dealers brought to the convention floor.

Physically, I was fine. If fact, thanks to a regimen of better eating, more sleep, and daily exercise I'd started a couple of years earlier, I was probably as physically fit as I'd been in a long time.

But mentally, I had grown dark.

I'm not fully sure what caused the clouds and malaise that settled on me.

Maybe I'd grown a little weary of the seemingly constant grind of travel to fulfill my responsibilities and work with Cox Automotive and vAuto.

Maybe it was my genetic disposition to worry, even if there wasn't always a good reason to get worked up about something.

Whatever the case, while dealers were riding high on the strength of ever-larger new and used vehicle sales gains, I began to sense that the stellar success of dealers using vAuto and the Velocity Method of Management had begun to sputter and maybe even wane.

My thinking drew in part from comments I'd begun hearing from dealers more and more frequently.

"Dale, we're selling cars like hotcakes, but I wish we were making more per copy."

"Dale, I know you've been talking and writing about margin compression, and it finally seems like it's arrived here in Des Moines."

"Dale, we had another record-setting month . . . but the grosses leave *a lot* to be desired."

These complaints and concerns were nothing new, particularly for car dealers who, like me, tend to always believe, or at least question, whether we could and should have made more money on a deal.

In many ways, the dealer complaints and concerns also seemed perfectly normal—the inevitable outcome of a market that, ever since the Internet came on the scene, had become more efficient, margin compressed, and transparent.

When dealers shared their concerns, I'd discuss how margin compression is a natural outcome of a more efficient market where consumer price discovery and the pursuit of a good deal represent a new normal.

In fact, I used the dealer concerns and complaints as inspiration.

At more and more speaking engagements with dealers and in my blog writing, I purposely focused on margin compression.

My goal was to help dealers better understand that while margin compression might be a condition of the current market, they most definitely could mitigate its effects by becoming more operationally efficient and turning inventory faster to maximize total profitability.

Still, the nagging in my mind needed answers.

I began to question if margin compression wasn't the only culprit. I began to wonder if something else might be making the condition of ever-smaller front-end gross profits more chronic for some dealers compared to others.

My search for answers sent me to NADA's financial data archive. I took a closer look at the period in question and immediately found two things:

First, there was some evidence that the industry's record-setting sales volumes came at the price of profit margins.

In new vehicles, for example, retail net profit per new vehicle retailed climbed out of the cellar between 2011 and 2012, rising from -$31 to $3, respectively. Dealers saw a significant increase in new vehicle sales in those two years, with the average dealership selling 682 vehicles in 2011 and 818 in 2012, according to NADA.

Then, as volumes grew even more, retail net profit went red again. By 2016, the industry's best-ever year in terms of new vehicle sales volumes, the average dealer was selling 928 new vehicles and making -$217 in retail net profit per new vehicle retailed.

I noticed a similar dynamic in used vehicles.

In 2011, dealers made an average retail net profit per used vehicle retailed of $203, while selling an average of 568 used vehicles per dealership. By 2016, dealers were retailing an average of 703 vehicles per dealership, but retail net profit per used vehicle retailed had dropped to $65.

After digging into these numbers, I felt a little better.

It seemed reasonable to think that the declines in net profit, in both new and used vehicles, owed to the classic trade-off in the car business: If you're going to go for volume, you're going to have to give up gross profit.

It seemed like maybe my worries were unfounded—until I saw NADA's dealership financial data for 2017.

It almost made my heart stop.

That year, according to NADA, the average retail net profit per new vehicle dropped to -$421 as dealers were essentially selling the same number of new cars.

Meanwhile, in used vehicles, the average retail net profit per vehicle retailed dropped to -$2, while Retail Sales Volumes essentially stayed the same.

At first, I wondered if the -$2 was a misprint. I was assured by folks at NADA that it wasn't. It was, in fact, the first time in the memories of everyone I know that dealers, as a whole, didn't yield any return from all the used vehicles they'd invested in and retailed.

I also learned that the -$2 net profit figure wasn't necessarily universal. In fact, the average owed largely to losses luxury dealers encountered as they worked through record numbers of lease returns their factory partners frequently forced them to purchase, often at amounts that exceeded current retail asking price averages.

Even so, I found myself worrying again.

CHAPTER 2

A STRETCH OF SERIOUS SOUL-SEARCHING

My deep dive into NADA financial data—and the steep drop in the average retail net profit per used vehicle retailed in 2017—left me scratching my head.

It didn't make sense to me that dealers would be *losing* money in used vehicles, particularly when they were still selling healthy numbers of cars year over year.

Even my dad, a retired Buick, GMC, and Cadillac dealer, found the figures hard to believe.

In his day, the used vehicle department was sometimes the only dealership profit center he could count on for cash flow and peace of mind.

I asked some of my economist friends for their input.

It just didn't seem right that dealers were suddenly on a fast track to not make any money in used vehicles. It also didn't seem like a more efficient and transparent market would trigger the dramatic change in retail net profits.

It was a puzzle I hoped my economist friends might help me figure out. We started our work with an even closer and deeper review of the NADA financial data.

We determined that the decline in the average retail net profit per used vehicle retailed had started around 2011. It happened in small increments—dropping $20 in 2012, $6 in 2013, and $7 in 2014.

We reasoned that these drops made perfect sense given that more and more used vehicle buyers were going online to find the best deal, and they had access to a wider array of resources that helped them pinpoint the best deal on their vehicle of choice.

The economists suggested that, for all intents and purposes, such diminishing returns from retail used vehicle sales were unsurprising signs of a market reaching a point of equilibrium.

But they were also struck by how, after a string of small declines, the average retail net profit per used vehicle retailed dropped by more than 50 percent between 2015 and 2016.

The economists thought there might be some merit to my instinctive sense, and felt that something so sudden might suggest an underlying problem or a shift in the used car business itself.

I enjoyed the conversations where the economists and I hypothesized about the factors that might be causing this situation.

Was it the record numbers of off-lease vehicles and related factory intervention?

A rise in the influence of "get the best deal" sites like CarGurus and TrueCar?

Could it be caused by more dealers adopting one-price or near-one-price strategies?

We'd go 'round and 'round the table, sipping bourbon and spitballing ideas.

Eventually, we agreed that each factor, in and of itself, couldn't possibly cause the dramatic drop in retail net profits.

Instead, the drop likely came from a confluence of all these factors, each of which gained considerable tailwind during the time in question.

We also agreed that maybe we were witnessing what amounted to a fundamental shift in the used vehicle market, and perhaps even a new normal.

From our armchair analyses, it seemed reasonable to conclude that the used vehicle business had arrived at a point where dealers could not simply sell more cars, even if they did so more efficiently, and expect to make a significant return on their investments.

But there was one factor I didn't disclose with my economist friends, despite the truth-telling effects of quality bourbon.

You see, I knew something about the used vehicle business that my economist friends didn't completely understand.

I knew that vAuto and the Velocity Method of Management had reached a critical mass at the same time used vehicle retail net profits suddenly went south.

I had started to wonder and worry whether Velocity itself, the principles of used vehicle management I had parented and

preached for years, might be part of the net profit problem, if
not the problem itself.

This was not a good time to be close or anywhere near me.

Just ask my wife, Nancy, or any one of my three sons.

Even my dad pulled me aside at a family dinner in 2017—a
fatherly check-in I didn't fully appreciate then but I fondly
recall today. He wanted to know if I was OK . . . and he suggested, in the same way he'd done when I was a teenager, that
it'd be best to lighten up around the family.

Dad was right, of course. I *was* crabby, cranky, and obsessed.
And it all came out at the worst times.

But my behavior was symptomatic of the fact that I was
troubled.

I simply had to know if there was any chance, even a remote
one, that I had been wrong, so ever f-ing wrong, about Velocity
and the transformative benefits I believed it brought to dealers
and the car business itself.

It was a serious stretch of soul-searching.

I'd lie awake at night thinking of all the dealers who had
asked me, almost from the first day I hit the road to sell vAuto,
the same question: "Dale, if everyone gets on vAuto, wouldn't
we all end up in a race to the bottom where nobody makes
any money?"

Looking back, I'd wonder if I had been too dismissive when
I answered the question.

My stock response to this dealer concern went something like this:

> Even if I gave vAuto away to every dealer, there would only be a handful who would actually use the system or use it properly.
>
> Individual dealers are so different and their used vehicle objectives so diffuse, that it simply isn't possible that the advent of a new software system and the Velocity Method of Management principles could or would cause such a disparate impact on the used vehicle market as a whole.

Every time I offered this response, I believed it to be true.

I'd even write about how Velocity adoption was like giving the same set of golf clubs to two different people.

Inevitably, the individuals would golf the way they knew best. They would not, nor could they, end up playing every hole the same way and seeing the exact same results, even if they used the same equipment.

But in late 2016 and into 2017, I also knew that vAuto and Velocity had become the predominate inventory management system for dealers in the US and Canada.

We had a sizable share of the market—which made me question whether those dealers who worried about a race to the bottom might be right about the cumulative effects of Velocity on the used vehicle business.

While there was no question that vAuto and Velocity had

made the used vehicle business a more profitable and success-ful pursuit for thousands of dealers over the years, it distressed me to think that our success might now be having the opposite effect on dealers.

I decided that the only way I might put my mind at ease would be to test the hypothesis—to drill down into the inventory data vAuto maintained on dealer inventories and apply a more critical eye to the dynamics the data might tell us about the used car business.

I'll be honest. I was worried and afraid of what I might find.

But I was driven by a sense of duty and obligation.

If something was wrong and if I'd had a role or any influence in its creation, then I bore a responsibility to at least identify the problem, if not find a solution.

The drill-down into vAuto data proved both affirming and alarming.

The data scientists and I discovered that, indeed, the used car business had changed, and not for the better.

What we found, in fact, represented bad news for every dealer, whether they used vAuto and followed Velocity principles or not.

CHAPTER 3

A REVELATION: A TROUBLING COST TO MARKET PROBLEM

I'm blessed to have a network of smart people in my personal and professional circle.

I make it a point to cultivate these relationships for a few reasons: These people help me think more deeply and sharply about the car business and how it may be changing for dealers. They keep me honest. They also help translate some of my ideas and thinking from abstract concepts to practical, usable solutions if there's merit.

One of these people is Chris Stutsman, who serves as senior director of product innovation for vAuto.

I first met Chris at Digital Motorworks in the mid-1990s as we were pioneering the technology that helped dealers send inventory data to sites like Autotrader and Cars.com.

Chris had come to Digital Motorworks a few months after

he'd graduated with a math degree from the University of Texas at Austin, after working a day job at a call-in help desk for a phone and wireless provider.

As Chris tells the story, he applied for the job at Digital Motorworks at the suggestion of a friend who'd recently started with the company. Chris had grown understandably tired of handling technical bugs brought to his attention by often-irate customers, while making little more than minimum wage.

During the Digital Motorworks interview, the hiring team asked Chris about his experience writing software code. Did he know SQL, the code or language used to ask and get information from a database?

"I told them I didn't know it but could learn it and take a test," Chris recalls. "But I thought they said 'Sequel.' It was only after I went to the bookstore and couldn't find the book that I realized they meant 'SQL.'"

Chris aced the test, and the interviewers decided to offer him the job. When the conversation got to money, they asked Chris about his salary expectations.

"I don't know," he says. "I want to make enough so that when I go out to eat, I can order a T-bone steak."

Naturally, Chris's nickname, T-Bone, was born, and it stayed with him through his tenure at Digital Motorworks and when he joined vAuto several years later.

I liked Chris right away.

He's a genuinely humble and nice person with a brilliant mind. He's also a quick study, as evidenced by his ability to learn SQL and the car business itself in short order.

With vAuto, Chris is one of the principal architects behind our inventory management solutions. He has a knack for translating abstract concepts and ideas into workable technology, as well as pushing back when an idea doesn't make sense or might only offer marginal value for dealers.

In 2017, when I knew that I needed to take a deeper dive into vAuto data to understand what might be different or wrong about the used car business and Velocity, I called T-Bone.

A FOCUS ON COST TO MARKET

Our initial conversations focused on the net profit declines we'd noticed in the NADA numbers.

We asked the same questions I'd batted around with my economist friends—why might this happen so suddenly and unexpectedly? What might be the best way to look at vAuto's inventory data to help us understand why the net profit declines were occurring?

Those queries led us to look deeply and critically at one of the foundational Velocity metrics—the Cost to Market percentage.

We landed on Cost to Market because it is the primary measure of opportunity and profit potential inherent in every used vehicle.

A quick bit of background on Cost to Market for those who don't know it: The Cost to Market metric measures the difference, or spread, between the cost required to own a vehicle and the average retail asking price for the vehicle in the current market.

For example, if a dealer purchases a vehicle for $8,500 and the prevailing average retail asking price for the unit is $10,000, the unit's Cost to Market percentage would be 85 percent. The image on this page shows the formula for calculating the Cost to Market percentage.

Cost to Market

$$\frac{\$8,500 \text{ owned}}{\$10,000 \text{ avg. retail asking price}} = 85\% \text{ Cost to Market}$$

For many years, vAuto Performance Managers and I coached dealers to do their best to maintain an overall Cost to Market percentage for their used vehicle inventories of 85 percent. This best practice owed to three factors:

First, we believed the Cost to Market percentage represented a better metric for understanding a vehicle's retail potential than the "cost up" method dealers had traditionally used to determine if an auction or trade-in purchase was "on the money."

The "cost up" method typically relied on wholesale book values or other wholesale references, like the Manheim Market Report, that don't always correlate or relate to the prevailing retail asking prices in local markets. For example, if you purchase a vehicle for $8,500 and know it to be "back of book," how useful is this insight if the prevailing retail price for the vehicle is $8,700?

Second, Cost to Market represented the industry's first objective measure of a used vehicle's retail potential. Under the "cost up" framework, dealers often had different opinions about whether the wholesale cost represented a good buy, as well as varying opinions on what the vehicle might fetch as a retail unit.

The Cost to Market metric effectively silences the debate. It simply is what it is.

When you know the Cost to Market percentage, you know the "spread," or front-end gross profit potential, that exists between your costs to own the vehicle and its average retail asking price.

Third, we knew that if we coached and preached the value of the Cost to Market metric and made sure it was always available in vAuto software, it would help dealers become more systematic about evaluating the retail profit potential for every vehicle. There'd be less guessing about a vehicle's front-end gross potential.

Over the years, we've been gratified to watch as dealers, armed with an understanding of each vehicle's Cost to Market percentage, have made better decisions about how they purchase, price, and merchandise their used vehicles to maximize their ability to make the "spread" they identified when they acquired a unit.

A DISTURBING FINDING

With our focus on Cost to Market percentages, Chris and I began to evaluate dealer inventory data in earnest.

Thankfully, we had a rich repository of data from more than 10,000 dealers across the United States for our analysis.

From our work with Velocity dealers, Chris and I knew that, on average, the Cost to Market percentage for dealer inventories and individual vehicles tends to go up over time.

This dynamic owes to changes in the retail market. A dealer's cost to own a vehicle doesn't change.

But the retail market changes all the time.

Competing cars come and go, and dealers typically make pricing adjustments, often lowering their asking prices as vehicles age in their inventories. These factors contribute to causing the Cost to Market percentages to climb over time.

You could view the rise in Cost to Market percentages as another way of measuring the reality of used vehicle depreciation that every dealer understands—time means money in the used vehicle business, and too much time can kill a vehicle's profit potential.

Through the years, I had come to understand that if a dealer owned a vehicle at a Cost to Market percentage of 85 percent on Day 1, it would likely reach a 90 percent Cost to Market percentage by the time it hit 60 days in inventory.

This upward movement in the Cost to Market percentage is a primary reason I've long advocated that dealers who believe they can own a vehicle for 90 to 120 days are probably not going to achieve the gross profit they would like to see, if there's any gross left at all when they retail the vehicle.

As Chris and I evaluated the Cost to Market data for dealer inventories, we found something that proved both surprising and disturbing—signs of what we came to understand as a gross deception.

Across the board, we noticed that sometime between 2016 and 2017—the same time frame that NADA's financial data showed a precipitous drop in the average retail net profit per used vehicle retailed—the time it took a vehicle to reach a Cost to Market percentage of 90 percent had essentially been cut in half.

That is, if it used to take 60 days for a vehicle to reach a Cost to Market percentage of 90 percent, our analysis showed that vehicles now hit this Cost to Market threshold in 30 to 45 days (see image at right).

VEHICLE INVENTORY FROM 2 YEARS AGO						CURRENT VEHICLE INVENTORY					
DAYS IN INVENTORY	COUNT	ADJ.% COST TO MARKET	AVG. MARKUP	ADJ.% PRICE TO MARKET	MKT. DAYS SUPPLY	DAYS IN INVENTORY	COUNT	ADJ.% COST TO MARKET	AVG. MARKUP	ADJ.% PRICE TO MARKET	MKT. DAYS SUPPLY
0-15	38	80%	$2,933	98%	60	0-15	38	88%	$2,193	98%	77
16-30	30	83%	$2,242	97%	64	16-30	30	89%	$1,377	97%	76
31-45	52	83%	$1,581	95%	64	31-45	52	90%	$315	96%	87
46-60	40	83%	$635	93%	70	46-60	40	93%	$326	96%	86
60+	39	90%	-$162	93%	69	60+	39	95%	-$76	95%	122
Total	199	83%	$2,010	95%	65	Total	199	91%	$1,072	97%	88

This insight brought an aha moment.

Ten years ago, I advocated that dealers should maintain at least 50 percent of their used vehicle inventories under 30 days of age specifically to minimize and mitigate the effects of the way Cost to Market percentages increase over time.

A couple of years ago, I began telling dealers that they should maintain at least 55 percent of their inventories under 30 days of age—a change to my benchmark recommendation that I made to help dealers struggling with making any money on their aged units.

I didn't realize, until Chris and I crunched the Cost to Market data, the new benchmark was a canary in a coal mine.

It was a signal that something fundamental had shifted in the used car business, thanks to the confluence of factors we discussed in the previous chapter.

Chris and I also used our analysis to test a question we were a little afraid to ask: To what extent did Velocity contribute to the Cost to Market appreciation problem?

Our analysis did not indict Velocity. There was, to borrow a phrase, no collusion.

But we would be kidding ourselves if we didn't call out Velocity as one of several market factors and forces that convened between 2016 and 2017.

Allow me to explain.

Between 2016 and 2017, vAuto reached a significant milestone as a company. We had more than 10,000 dealers in the US and Canada using our Provision software.

At the same time, there were at least a handful of other used vehicle inventory management providers in the market.

While there are significant differences in the methodologies and systems that inventory management providers bring to dealers, this period marked a time when you would have been hard-pressed to find a dealer who didn't:

a) have a pricing strategy that sought to optimize each vehicle's competitive market price position, and

b) have someone, if not themselves, who came to work each day knowing that if they wanted to retail more used vehicles in the go-go market of the time, they'd need to pay closer attention to their pricing.

In other words, you had a market where an ever-growing emphasis on market-based pricing could not be ruled out as a contributing factor to the faster rise in Cost to Market percentages.

Chris and I went a step further as we investigated Velocity's possible contribution to the changes in Cost to Market percentages: We compared the Cost to Market data between vAuto and non-vAuto dealers to see if there was any difference.

Here's what we found:

The appreciation in Cost to Market percentages varies from dealer to dealer and market to market. It's a bigger problem in highly competitive metro and midsized markets than in more rural areas. It also seems to be highly problematic for dealers who retail higher-dollar luxury vehicles.

The data differences between vAuto and non-vAuto dealers were negligible.

This insight brought some relief.

Chris and I felt more comfortable that vAuto and Velocity did not have any outsize influence on Cost to Market trends than anyone else. It seemed like the faster rate of Cost to Market appreciation truly reflected an industry-wide problem.

Chris and I noticed something else as we examined the inventory data: The acceleration of Cost to Market percentages seemed to be creating a situation where, even if dealers turned their used vehicles faster, it wouldn't be enough to compensate for the ever-smaller margins.

We both did a double-take when we recognized that

ever-faster inventory turns seemed to be less effective as an anti-
dote to margin compression.

It was at that moment that Chris and I began to think long
and hard about how dealers could effectively contend with the
industry-wide Cost to Market appreciation problem.

We realized that, at its most basic level, we were looking at a
math problem that needed to be solved.

CHAPTER 4

THE NEW MATH OF THE USED CAR BUSINESS

A s vAuto's Chris Stutsman and I set out to identify how dealers could better contend with the faster Cost to Market appreciation we identified, we dubbed the effort the "New Math of the Used Car Business."

We started by formulating what we knew about the Cost to Market problem.

We'd found that across virtually every used vehicle inventory in the country, dealers faced the same predicament: Somewhere between 30 and 45 days in inventory, most vehicles lose their ability to make a significant contribution to the used vehicle department's bottom line.

We also noted that, in many cases, the cars that age past the 30- to 45-day threshold represent a net loss when they retail.

Consider this example: Let's say you paid $20,000 to own

and recondition a vehicle. You've had it in your inventory for 45 days, and its Cost to Market percentage is now 90 percent.

In most cases, this vehicle will not transact, or leave your inventory, at a Price to Market percentage of 100 percent. (For those who don't know, the Price to Market metric measures where a vehicle's retail price point stands in relation to the market average for the same/similar vehicles. An example: If your used vehicle is priced at $9,500 and the market average is $10,000, the vehicle would have a Price to Market percentage of 95 percent.)

In most cases, the $20,000 vehicle will transact at a Price to Market percentage between 91 and 94 percent.

Let's say you retail the vehicle at a Price to Market percentage of 93 percent. The transaction would translate to a $600 front-end gross profit, which represents the 3 percent spread between your Cost to Market and Price to Market percentages.

For most dealers, the $600 would be a less than satisfying return on the $20,000 investment. Many would probably also reconcile their disappointment with the fact that at least they didn't lose money on the deal. It generated $600 for their used vehicle department and generated additional gross in F&I and service.

But here's the gross deception dealers typically don't see.

Once dealers pay a salesperson's commission and allocate departmental expenses to the vehicle, the transaction represents a net loss for the used vehicle department's bottom line. The addition of these expenses effectively wipes out the $600 gross profit the dealers thought they made when they sold the vehicle.

As I share the reality of the new math with dealers, they nod their heads. The logic and the math seem to make sense.

But they often don't fully believe what I'm telling them.

That's when I'll encourage them to take a closer look at their own inventories—to look at the Cost to Market percentages on vehicles that are 45 days old and older, and then evaluate whether the retail sales of these vehicles and the gross profits the deals produced amounted to a positive ROI or net profit on their financial statements.

This investigation usually serves as a wake-up call and a warning.

The wake-up call arrives when dealers realize that, while they know the number of vehicles they sell every month, the average front-end gross profits, and the units they have in stock, they aren't aware of what I'd argue is the most important metric of all: the net profit a vehicle produces.

I'm sometimes shocked and surprised that dealers, and especially their managers, aren't aware of how bad the net profitability in used vehicle departments has become.

On some level, I suppose, the lack of net profit awareness makes some sense. After all, dealers have enjoyed a long run, making good money in used vehicles. They haven't had to pay close attention to the department's net profit. In years past, you could simply sell vehicles and count on making money.

That's why the New Math of Used Vehicles serves as a warning. It suggests that if dealers *do not* pay more attention to the net profits their used vehicle departments produce, they'll face an increasingly rude awakening when they do.

Looking back at the NADA numbers in the context of our analysis, Chris and I estimated that half of the used vehicle departments in the country were in the black in 2017, while the others lost money.

I certainly remember the early days of 2019, when I heard multiple comments from dealers who were incredulous about their used vehicle losses, even as they were selling more cars than ever.

"Dale, I don't understand it. We sold a record number of used vehicles last year, but we lost money in our used vehicle department. It doesn't make any sense."

I'd have to agree.

It doesn't make any sense unless and until you recognize and understand the truth about the New Math of Used Cars and how much your current inventory management methods and processes do not account for its far shorter retail timeline for most vehicles.

But here's the good news.

Just as there's a specific order of operations for solving math problems, there's a specific way dealers can make the New Math work in their used vehicle departments.

Let's have a look in the next chapter.

CHAPTER 5

BALANCING THE NEW MATH EQUATION

Thirty years ago, when I was a Cadillac dealer and you asked me what I did for a living, I would have told you, "I sell cars."

If you asked the same question of dealers and managers today, I'd bet good money that you'd basically get the same answer: "I sell cars."

It's the classic response of the car guys and car gals who serve in the ranks of retail automotive.

Selling cars isn't just what we do, it's who we are.

I still self-identify as a car guy, even though I haven't sold one in 30 years.

My dad's the same.

He's 93 and still going strong. He'll be the first to tell you he's a car guy who made a good living selling cars.

But with the rise of the New Math and the lack of industry

awareness about its damaging effects on used vehicle department profitability, dealers need to recognize that their primary purpose in the used vehicle department isn't to sell cars, it's to make money.

Now, some might consider this a moot or even silly point.

They might argue that dealers and managers are, and always have been, focused on making money when they sell cars.

That's why they put the screws on customers to hold gross, or try to steal trade-ins. Some might take the argument further, suggesting there are plenty of dealers and managers who focus *too much* on making money.

These folks will point to the less than favorable Customer Satisfaction Index (CSI) scores and negative online reviews some dealers receive as ample evidence.

But this view misses the broader point—which is that selling used cars in today's environment of market efficiency, transparency, and the New Math is no longer a sure-fire method of making money.

It hasn't always been this way, of course.

There was a time, not so long ago, when you could almost guarantee that if you stocked a used vehicle, you'd eventually sell it and make money.

You could have a vehicle remain on your lot for 60, 75, or 90 days, and you could expect to make money.

That's because in those days not so long ago, you could also expect that a vehicle's Cost to Market percentage wouldn't reach 90 percent until 90 days or so in inventory.

But we've already established the retail timeline for the average used vehicle is much shorter.

Today, the Cost to Market percentage of many used vehicles reaches 90 percent in 30 to 45 days, and in some cases 15 days.

With this new reality, it's no longer sufficient to believe that you can stock cars, wait for them to sell, and expect a satisfying amount of used vehicle net profit.

With the rise of the New Math, selling used cars and making money no longer go automatically hand in hand.

That's why I believe it's critically important that dealers and managers rethink their primary responsibility and role in used vehicles—your job isn't just to sell cars, it's to *make money*.

This new identity and job description require stepping away from the deception that selling cars and making gross equate to making money—and stepping into a new way of managing and retailing used vehicles that prioritizes each unit's net profit and ROI potential.

A STOCKING RATIO PROBLEM

Perhaps the most evident sign that dealers and managers are not as investment- or money-minded as they could be with used vehicles relates to the size of their inventories in relation to their retail sales.

When I was a dealer, we stocked our used vehicle inventory like everyone else: If we sold 50 cars, we'd keep at least 100 in stock.

I didn't think much of this 2:1 stock-to-sell ratio. It's what I'd learned as a best practice. It's the same ratio my dad followed in all his years in the business.

It's a practice that owed to a collective belief that our primary job in used vehicles is to sell cars. And if you're going to sell cars, you've got to stock a sufficient supply so you have enough to sell.

Even with the rise of Velocity management, the practice of stocking more cars than you sell remains prevalent.

In fact, I'd assert that some dealers who might have aimed for a more efficient stock-to-sell ratio of 1:1 years ago have eased off, fattening up as retail sales have improved and returning to a 2:1 stock-to-sell ratio.

But here's the problem.

The 2:1 stock-to-sell ratio is out of balance with the New Math and its faster pace of Cost to Market appreciation.

There's no question in my mind that at least part of the reason NADA reports a steady decline in the average retail net profit per used vehicle retailed owes to the fact that dealers are carrying too much inventory for too long.

As a result, dealers are retailing too many vehicles where the Cost to Market percentage has climbed past 90 percent, and when these deals hit the bottom line, they often amount to losses in net profit.

All this begs a critical question: OK, Dale, I get it. Vehicles are losing profit potential faster, and I probably have too much inventory in stock. What's the fix?

The fix, in my view, ties directly to the balance between the number of vehicles you stock and the number you sell.

As an industry, dealers need to make a significant shift from a "stock to sell" to a "sell to stock" operational mentality.

This mindset shift is a first step in balancing the New Math equation in a used vehicle department.

Next, dealers need to recognize that if you want to stock more vehicles, you must earn the right to do so by selling the cars you have first.

Unless and until the balance between the number of vehicles you stock and retail occurs, I don't think dealers can or should expect to see a satisfying net profit or ROI for their used vehicle departments.

In fact, if dealers let the imbalance linger, they're making a conscious decision to lose money in their used vehicle departments.

That's because you can't fight the New Math.

It's unrelenting. If you stock more vehicles than you sell, you'll automatically ensure that at least some percentage of your inventory will age to 45 or 60 days, and they'll carry the stain of a Cost to Market percentage that's 90 percent or better.

Sure, you'll eventually retail those older-age units.

But you won't make any money, even if the deal generates a small front-end gross profit. By the time these sales hit the bottom line, they'll amount to a loss that, in turn, diminishes all the other front-end gross profit you were rightfully proud to earn.

Let me put it another way: If you were retailing fresh fish instead of used vehicles, you'd be much more inclined to stock your coolers with a just-right supply of fish.

If you regularly chose to stock more than you sold, you would know it'd be a losing game. You'd constantly end up writing off the loss of rotten fish against your profits.

Unfortunately, that's the point we've reached in used vehicles, thanks to the New Math.

It has raised the urgency by which dealers should adopt the money-making strategy of aligning the size of their inventories to the number of retail sales they put on the books.

A NEW MANAGEMENT METRIC: YOUR ROLLING 30-DAY TOTAL OF RETAIL SALES

As I help dealers balance the New Math equation, I'll recommend that they add a new metric to their inventory management tool kit—the rolling 30-day total retail sales count.

It's interesting when I ask dealers to share this number.

Most have no idea what I'm talking about. They'll rattle off their sales volume from the prior month or how they're positioned to meet the current month's goal.

But they don't know the rolling 30-day total retail sales count without looking it up.

The blank stares suggest that the rolling 30-day total retail sales count should be as fundamental to managing a used vehicle department as your front-end gross profit, your current and last month's sales, and the size of your inventory.

This new metric needs to be understood as a primary lever, or mechanism, that dealers can use to make money, not just sell cars, in their used vehicle departments.

Here's how the metric should be put in practice to balance the New Math equation and cut a path to increased profitability:

Calculate the metric: You determine your rolling 30-day total of retail sales by counting back 30 days from yesterday and tallying up the retail sales. Tomorrow, you'll drop off the 31st day and add today's retail sales to the total.

Apply the metric: Once you know your rolling 30-day total of retail sales, compare the number to your total number of vehicles you have in inventory, whether they are front-line ready or not.

Do the numbers match up?

If the answer is yes, then you have balanced the equation and set the stage to make the New Math work in your used vehicle department.

If the answer is no, and you have more vehicles than you are retailing, then you must put a stop on the proactive acquisition of inventory from auctions or other wholesale sources. You have not yet sold enough vehicles to earn the right to acquire more cars.

BUT if your inventory suffers from an imbalance between your rolling 30-day total of retail sales and your current inventory, you *should not* stop acquiring trade-in vehicles.

That's because both your new and used vehicle departments rely on trade-ins to keep retail sales—and the "wheel of fortune" a used vehicle sale creates across dealership departments—moving.

The restriction on acquiring cars relates to auction vehicles. Unless you have clear evidence that your inventory levels are less than your rolling 30-day total, you shouldn't go out and acquire auction vehicles because you "need some cars."

If you do, I believe you are effectively choosing to commit corporate capital to an investment that will more than likely generate a loss in net profit.

Remember: If you're stocking more cars than you're selling,

you're setting yourself up for retail deals that will result in losses in retail net profit and will diminish your used vehicle department's overall profitability.

Keep the metric close: In today's era of the New Math, dealers need to have their rolling 30-day total of retail sales top of mind. You have to know it. You can't look it up.

The metric must be a part of your day-to-day decision making, just like the other metrics—average front-end gross, current monthly sales, total inventory count, average retail net profit per used vehicle retailed, etc.—you use to manage your inventory.

You'll need to know the rolling 30-day total of retail sales and have it handy because your effort to maintain a more efficient inventory-to-sales ratio will meet resistance. And sometimes, it'll be stiff.

If you're a dealer, you'll hear it from your managers. "Boss, we aren't selling cars because we don't have the cars to sell."

If you're a manager, you'll hear it from your salespeople. "Boss, I can't make any money if I don't have fresh cars to sell."

In today's era of the New Math, such comments are distractions from the real purpose of every used vehicle department—to put the primary focus on making money, which means generating a positive ROI and net profit, and not just selling cars.

I've been spending considerable time helping dealers balance the New Math equation in their used vehicle departments. In chapter 7, I'll share the story of a dealer who has balanced the equation and is enjoying increased sales volumes *and* net profitability.

But first, I need to address a question that's likely lingering in the minds of many readers: If you can't stock cars to sell cars, how can you effectively grow your sales volumes?

I'll attempt to answer that question now.

CHAPTER 6

PUSHBACK ON THE BALANCED NEW MATH EQUATION

Some dealers get upset when I share my perspective to balance the New Math equation in their used vehicle departments.

They automatically assume that my prescription to align retail sales with inventory levels robs them of the single most effective lever they can pull to increase used vehicle sales volumes—putting more cars on the lot.

The dealers are correct. My prescription does take away what has become understood as an easy, fast, and relatively reliable way for dealers to build used vehicle sales volumes.

But the takeaway is necessary.

That's because simply adding more cars to your inventory doesn't offer a way to profitably increase sales volumes, thanks to the rise of the New Math and the faster rate of Cost to Market appreciation.

In fact, if you add more inventory to grow sales volumes, you'll probably end up retailing an even larger number of vehicles that, when you pay out a commission and charge departmental expenses to the transaction, result in a loss for retail net profit.

This reality begs the question: If you can't take the easy route and add more inventory to sell more cars, what is the best way to increase sales volumes and ensure that your growth doesn't come at the expense of your profitability?

The answer is that there are several ways dealers can increase sales volumes.

To be sure, none of them is as easy as the tried-and-true "go buy some cars" method.

But each of the following is a fundamentally legitimate and sound way to increase sales volumes as you balance the New Math equation:

1. **IMPROVE YOUR PRICING EFFICIENCY.** On any given day, at most dealerships there are several vehicles that fit into a "needs attention" category due to their pricing. This occurs when a vehicle's asking price is missing or it has fallen out of alignment with the vehicle's competitive set or the parameters of your pricing strategy.

    > In many instances, the "needs attention" vehicles owe directly to a lack of attention on the part of a dealer or used vehicle manager.

> As dealers and their teams work to minimize these pricing inefficiencies, they find that vehicles tend to retail faster. In turn, as dealers retail these vehicles, they earn the right to acquire another one, a cycle that helps dealers achieve their goal of sales volume growth.

2. **SHARPEN YOUR FOCUS ON ACQUISITIONS.** I have never met a dealer or used vehicle manager who didn't at least suspect, if not believe, that they could do a better job buying cars. This is true even among those who, in their heart of hearts, believe they're doing everything in their power to make the best possible auction and trade-in purchases.

> When you work to balance the New Math, though, it's imperative to move from thinking you could do a better job to actually doing it. Every car counts a little more when you align your inventory sales levels to your rolling 30-day retail sales total.
>
> This important work starts with the recognition and belief that your market is your best guide. It can tell you what's selling in your market, what's selling fast, and what will probably take awhile to retail without some hands-on intervention.
>
> By applying these insights as you acquire used vehicles, dealers and managers go beyond just balancing the equation. They are balancing their inventory portfolios to the vehicle segments and price groups that sell best in their market. As a result, the dealers

consistently stock the right mix of cars their customers will want to bring home, which drives sales volumes.

It's no different than an investment-optimized soda vending machine.

If Diet Coke's the best seller, you can bet the machine's owner will make sure the brand doesn't run out. Similarly, if Dr. Pepper's a so-so seller, the owner won't oversupply the machine with Dr. Pepper, which would tie up capital in an underperforming investment and slow the return it might generate.

3. **REDUCE YOUR RECONDITIONING TIMES.** Even the best cars get a bad start if it takes you more than three days to get them online and retail ready. Industry stats suggest the average time it takes dealers to get their used vehicles reconditioned runs between seven and 10 days. The more time a vehicle takes for reconditioning, the less time you've got to maximize its profit and retail potential. Typically, a faster reconditioning throughput means a faster pace of retail sales, which helps sales volumes grow.

4. **INCREASE YOUR MARKETING/MERCHANDISING EFFECTIVENESS.** The asking price attention gap noted above has a first cousin—the amount of time dealers and managers focus on how well they market and merchandise their used vehicles. To be sure, dealers and managers are 10x better at managing their online listings than they were not long ago. They know that Vehicle Details Page (VDP) views are indicators of future retail sales.

> But there's room for better oversight of VDP engage-
> ment and the use of tools to increase visibility for spe-
> cific vehicles when they need it that can help dealers
> increase sales volumes.

5. **MAKE YOUR SALES PROCESS MORE EFFICIENT.** Cox Automotive's annual Buyer Journey Study has shown a consistent
decline in the time that new and used vehicle buyers are
spending to research their next vehicle. The decline owes to
the better information vehicle buyers can now find online
and their collective, growing comfort in sussing out the
particulars of a purchase, even a new or used vehicle, from
home, work, or anywhere else they choose.

> But here's the question: Over the past three years,
> has the time you require of customers to purchase a
> vehicle declined?
>
> The best answer would be, "Yes, and we're invest-
> ing in digital retailing technology and tools that can
> help buyers complete as much of the deal with us
> online as they want."
>
> It shouldn't be a stretch for anyone in the car busi-
> ness to see that if it takes less time to sell a car, you
> should be able to sell more cars.
>
> Similarly, I don't think it's a stretch to say that if
> the time you require of customers to purchase vehi-
> cles has not declined, that might be a reason you
> haven't been able to grow sales volumes as much
> as you'd like.

Dealers who diligently work to balance the New Math equation and pursue one or more of these objectives in earnest will be on their way to increasing sales volumes by earning the right to stock more vehicles as they retail more cars.

But I should underscore an earlier point: None of these methods represents a fast or easy way to achieve the objective of increasing sales volumes.

Each requires time. Each requires training and retraining. Each requires the discipline, patience, and will of dealers and their managers to achieve a positive end result.

Furthermore, none of these methods to increase sales volumes will help you achieve the primary objective of your used vehicle department—which is to achieve positive net profit—unless and until you balance the New Math equation and establish the foundation for profit-generating retail sales.

For example, you can spend all kinds of energy, resources, and time on trimming the time it takes to sell a car.

But it won't do you much good if your sales associates are being asked to sell cars that won't make any money for them or for your used vehicle department. Their disappointment has a tendency to carry through and cloud even the most convenient and efficient sales process.

It's a little bit of a double-edged sword—unless and until you balance the New Math, your efforts to grow sales volumes, and do so profitably, won't see the level of success you desire and your dealership deserves.

The good news is that there are dealers who've been there, done the dirty work, and agreed to tell their stories.

Let's have a look at one of them.

CHAPTER 7

BALANCING THE NEW MATH EQUATION: FROM HOCKEY TO FIGURE SKATING

Bill Knight of Tulsa, OK–based Bill Knight Automotive has a unique view of his responsibility as the leader of his dealerships.

He's like a barrel man on the sailing ships of old—perched high in the crow's nest, a spyglass trained on the horizon and seas ahead.

"My job is to look around the corner," says Knight, a majority owner of three stores in Oklahoma and a minority owner of one in California. "It's my job to make sure the team understands what's coming ahead of us, because some of the weakness we have in the business is because we're so focused on today."

Knight's efforts to define and divine future challenges and opportunities led him to a profoundly disturbing observation about two years ago.

"I had started to see a lot of pressure on front-end gross, and a lot of differences in the marketplace," he says. "We had a 90-day soft turn in used vehicles. We were always able to get out. Somebody would come in and buy the car, and we'd sometimes make money. It was very rare that we would get in trouble on a car.

"But that's what I saw start to change—our ability to get out of that car in 60 days. That's where we had our head buried in the sand," Knight says. "That's when I realized something is fundamentally different."

While he didn't know it at the time, Knight had started to observe what I've come to call the New Math of the Used Car Business. He had spotted the fact that his net profits in used vehicles had begun to head south. He worried that he might start seeing the same net profit losses as other dealers.

He realized that the way he and his team were managing their used vehicle departments wasn't working as well as it had in the past.

"We've been negative net selling new cars for some time," Knight says. "It was a great wake-up call when I started to see used cars get painted with the same brush. That was the case for change. That was the motivation to break what we've done and start over."

It was around this time that I began to work with Knight and his team. I'd met Knight through Alex Taylor, Cox Automotive's CEO and great-grandson of company founder, James M. Cox, a former governor of Ohio and newspaper publisher.

I offered to host monthly calls to review the used vehicle performance and profitability at Knight's dealerships.

He agreed, and we went to work.

A JOURNEY TO BALANCE THE NEW MATH EQUATION

I remember the first few meetings with Knight and his team.

We talked at length about how his stores appeared to be saddled with a sizable share of aged inventory, which owed to a few factors:

First, like many dealers, Knight and his team maintained a 60- to 70-day supply of inventory on the ground. It had been a long-standing practice, one that remains in line with recommendations from NADA, 20 Groups, and other industry sources.

In simple terms, the 60- to 70-day supply of inventory meant that Knight had twice as many used vehicles on the ground every month than the number they sold.

Add in the group's 90-day soft turn policy, and you've got a recipe that tends to produce an outsize share of older-age inventory.

Second, while Knight's managers understood the importance of getting vehicles in/out of reconditioning and getting descriptions, photos, and prices posted as quickly as possible, their day-to-day decisions and processes produced less-than-efficient outcomes.

Recon times often ran up to seven days or more, and it might take a few more days to get vehicles fully merchandised and priced online.

As Knight and his team took a closer look at their performance, they realized they had significant room for improvement.

"When we had our first meeting with Dale, some of the guys felt like, 'Yeah, we're doing that' or 'We got that,'" Knight recalls. "As we got into it more deeply, we realized we weren't doing it and didn't have it.

"It's all cause and effect," he adds. "You can't do certain things that it takes to be successful if the other systems aren't working. One by one, we'd begin to take our processes apart and put them back together again."

Knight reiterates the effort wasn't easy. It took time before he and his team started to see some improvement in the speed and efficiency of their used vehicle management processes.

But Knight also felt something was missing—and he found it when one of his managers brought up the idea of buying more inventory to sell more vehicles.

I stopped the conversation.

I reiterated how the New Math of Used Cars has effectively broken the tradition-bound idea that dealers can stock cars to sell cars.

I suggested that Knight and his team would be better off if they first worked to balance the New Math Equation, maintaining used vehicle inventory levels based on each store's rolling 30-day retail sales total.

I explained that in today's market, dealers must earn the right to stock more used vehicles by retailing the ones they already have in stock.

"That's when the light bulb went on," Knight says. "It gave me a tool I'd been looking for—a way to hold everyone accountable to sustain the things we were doing to become more efficient and profitable. It was a big moment. I realized that's how we should do it."

That's how Knight and his team began their journey to balance the New Math Equation.

He will be the first to tell you—it's a tough thing to do when you've been conditioned, taught, and trained for so long to essentially stock twice as many vehicles as you retail in a given month.

The balancing effort began by pricing the older-age inventory to retail quickly—a clearing of the table, if you will, to set the stage for healthier ROI and net profits.

It was a painful time. The retail sales of the older-age units often brought losses and financial pain for team members who get paid off the gross profit the used vehicle department generates.

"There was some pain," Knight affirms. "The dealership felt it. The managers felt it. I told my team, 'Look, we've been in the business together long enough. We're going to own this together.'"

There was also doubt about the group's new direction.

"My guys would ask, 'Why are we doing this?' and 'Aren't things fine?'" Knight says. "I told them, things *were* fine for 2017. But they won't be fine for 2020. We were fixing a net profit problem that had started to develop and clearly was going to get worse if we didn't address it."

The group's efforts to balance the New Math Equation brought a renewed commitment and focus to ensuring operational efficiencies in the used vehicle department and beyond.

"The thing I love about running a rolling 30-day total inventory is it's hard. It's difficult. But it puts pressure in all the right places," Knight says. "That's what gravitated me to the idea. It makes you do everything from Day 1. You can't wait until the end."

Through a lot of coaching and effort, Knight and his team have balanced the New Math Equation. Their inventory levels now run in line with their rolling total of retail sales in the past 30 days.

They have trimmed the time it takes to get vehicles reconditioned, priced, and posted online. They are paying closer attention to the vehicles once they're listed online, checking more frequently for online interest and reviewing prices twice a week.

Today, the commitment and effort Knight and his team have invested in balancing the New Math equation are bearing fruit.

Sales volumes are improving. Knight's Ford store in Stillwater, for example, has doubled its monthly sales volumes to 70 vehicles. His Ford store in Tulsa has added another 20 units to its monthly sales, and his Lincoln/Volvo store is on pace to see volume improvement.

Gross profits are improving, too. Knight says, "They aren't where they were two years ago, but that's true for everyone."

Inventories are also cleaner than they've ever been. "If our used car business is an A- today, it was probably a B- before," Knight says.

"But what has changed is the cleanliness of the inventory," he notes. "Using a rolling 30-day total of sales for your inventory levels really does take the focus off age, because it makes age go away. You can't have a rolling 30-day total and have aged cars."

Knight's group is now facing another challenge that arrives once you've balanced the New Math equation—how to grow sales volumes while maintaining, if not increasing, the front-end gross and net profitability improvements they've enjoyed.

Knight says profit-minded growth is possible, but it's not as easy as buying a truckload of used vehicles.

Instead, it's a series of calculated efforts to add more vehicles when they've earned the right to do so.

"You go buy an extra five or three or six vehicles and, if our process is working right, we can handle and work our way through them without losing momentum."

He notes that sourcing vehicles (a topic that we'll address in chapters 14 and 21) is becoming more critical, given softer new vehicle sales is slowing the influx of trade-ins that feed his inventories.

Overall, Knight is happy with the direction his team is headed and the performance of his used vehicle department teams.

By balancing the New Math equation, "I'm promoting the right behavior, and that's a big deal for me," Knight says. "The 30-day rolling inventory cap keeps everyone focused on the right stuff. It can't be manipulated. You can't sell more unless you do the right stuff, and you can't get more inventory unless you sell more."

In addition, Knight sleeps easier at night.

"The rolling 30-day approach reduces the worry we all have in the middle of the night about the amount of money we have tied up in inventory," he says. "When I can turn my inventory up to 18 times a year, that's just better.

"In a business where margin compression is happening all over, and business expenses are up, the rolling 30-day total removes your used car department from being a drag on inventory and turn to becoming the star of the show."

Knight's story is a realistic, shining example of how balancing the New Math equation at dealerships serves as a predicate for positive ROI and net profit improvement in used vehicle departments.

It's worth underscoring a point that Knight shared several times—it's not an easy shift, and it's more difficult when your teams are firmly tied to traditional used vehicle management practices.

"It's like we're ice hockey players and we need to learn to be figure skaters," Knight says. "It's change management, and it takes a lot of trust to get the buy-in you need."

We'll take a closer look at change management tips from Knight and other dealers in chapter 22.

In the meantime, let's return to the work vAuto's Chris Stutsman and I were doing to better understand the role of time and money in used vehicle management—and how both have become a gross deception for dealers.

CHAPTER 8

A QUESTION OF TIME AND MONEY IN USED CARS

One of the most wonderful aspects of my job for Cox Automotive is that I have the latitude, luxury, and time to satisfy my curiosity.

Without this blessing, the discovery about the New Math and the faster appreciation of Cost to Market percentages in used cars would not have happened.

We also would not have been able to quantify for the industry how this shift in the money-making fundamentals of the used vehicle business had occurred, let alone devise a way for dealers to balance the New Math equation at their dealerships.

Through all this work, I began to zero in on the fact that our findings essentially revealed that time was moving faster and faster in used vehicles.

I began to ponder whether, thanks to margin compression,

market efficiency, price transparency, and other factors, time might eventually run out on used vehicles themselves—that the industry might arrive at a time when dealers wouldn't make any money retailing a used vehicle, much like the unfortunate loss leader–like reality in new vehicle departments these days.

This road to ruin didn't make any sense to me on several levels.

First, there's a rule that says markets, over time, eventually find equilibrium.

The equilibrium often arrives after disruption forces a significant change in a business sector that produces a shakeout. The shakeout typically involves the loss of businesses that fail to adapt to the new, often more efficient and bottom-line-challenged realities of a changed business model.

Think of books.

I loved going to Border's. At its peak, Border's was a destination for my family and me.

Once we got to the store, we'd all scatter. Each of us headed to a favorite section. You'd inevitably find me in the music section, listening to all kinds of new and old music. Later, we'd all gather to talk about what we'd purchased or seen, while sitting at the café, enjoying a snack.

But for all its charms, Border's couldn't survive the rise of Amazon and the more convenient, cost-effective way to buy books and music that it brought to the market.

The market equilibrium that's followed has not been good for brick-and-mortar bookstores. But they're still around, often with a more boutique-style approach to their retail spaces and stock on the shelves.

I think it's fair to say the used car business is still finding its equilibrium.

The disruption that's come from ever-greater market efficiency, price awareness, and transparency continues to corrode the underlying financials of used vehicle departments across the country.

I regard the NADA-reported declines in average retail net profit per used vehicle retailed and the New Math of the Used Vehicle Business as Exhibits "A" and "B" of this ongoing disruption.

Many dealers are also seeing tangible signs of this fallout right down the street or in the next town over.

As I'm writing in the early fall of 2019, more dealers report that they're seeing nearby dealerships, often independent but sometimes franchise competitors, either selling out or shutting down.

The problem, I believe, is that these dealers either chose not to reckon with the change in the underlying financial fundamentals and margins of retailing new and used vehicles, or they tried and failed to make the transition.

Conversely, I'm aware of many dealers who are doing just fine, thank you. Their secret seems to be an even greater focus on efficiency in the way they manage their capital and day-to-day business operations. It should also be noted that, by and large, these dealers maintain a fairly close 1:1 ratio between their used vehicle inventories and their rolling 30-day totals of retail sales.

When I consider these dynamics, it seems to me that the used car business is moving toward a state of equilibrium, but perhaps it hasn't arrived there just yet.

Beyond market equilibrium, it also troubled me that the pace of net profit declines in used vehicles might owe to something other than just the rise of market efficiency, price awareness, and transparency.

As I noted in chapter 2, my economist friends and I reasoned that a steady drop in dealer margins would seem to be the normal course of a business undergoing a decade-long disruption and finding its equilibrium.

I began to wonder if perhaps the dramatic and sudden changes in used vehicle net profitability might owe to a deficiency in the way dealers were managing their used vehicle departments.

That's when vAuto's Chris Stutsman and I began dismantling and dissecting the two foremost drivers of virtually every significant used vehicle management decision—time in inventory and front-end gross profit.

TIME: A CORNERSTONE OF CONSEQUENTIAL USED CAR DECISIONS

If we were to take the time to stop and think about time, I think everyone would agree that it's perhaps the single most important driver of our day-to-day decisions.

Here's a snapshot from my world:

When I go to bed at night, I generally consider what time I should get up the next morning, given the time of the first family commitment or work to-do on my calendar.

When I'm thinking about what to eat for breakfast, I'll

consider when I'm likely to eat again, and choose something I expect to sustain me during the time between the two meals.

If someone asks me for a call or conversation, I'll often ask how much time we'll need and the best time to put it on my calendar.

When I get dressed, I'll consider whether what I wear is appropriate for the people, places, and times of day I'll be out and about, as well as my own age (a problem, apparently, when there's a party on the family schedule).

Time is also a fascination, and even a bit mysterious for us as human beings.

There's Albert Einstein's study of relativity and the space-time continuum, which TV shows like *Star Trek: Next Generation* turned into a household term.

Musical artists often sing and write about time—"Time Is on My Side" (Rolling Stones); "Time" (Pink Floyd); "Time in a Bottle" (Jim Croce); "Funny How Time Slips Away" (Willie Nelson); "One More Time" (Joe Jackson); "Time After Time" (Cyndi Lauper); "Too Much Time on My Hands" (Styx).

We talk all the time about the healing power of time ("Don't worry, time heals all wounds" or "You'll feel better in time"), its speed in passing ("Geez, where did the time go?" or "Man, this day is dragging on forever"), and, especially these days, its scarcity ("Sorry, I just don't have the time").

But when you consider the influence and role that time plays in used vehicle management, it's much more than a fascination; it's foundational.

If you think about it, every decision of consequence a dealer makes about a used vehicle, at any point in its life cycle, inherently has a consideration for or an element of time in it.

Should I acquire this car? When dealers and managers make this decision, they're implicitly, if not explicitly, thinking whether they'll be able to retail the vehicle in a given amount of time, which is usually expressed as days on the calendar.

How much should I pay for the car? When dealers answer this question, they're considering a number that includes an estimate of the front-end gross profit they'll likely make and the amount of time it'll take for them to make it.

How should I price a car? In most if not all cases, dealers set the initial asking price of a vehicle based on factors that include whether it's a "fresh" car.

How much should I change the price of the car? These decisions are rooted in time, too. In many cases, the size of the price reduction or price increase depends on how long, or how many days, a vehicle has been in a dealer's inventory.

When should I get rid of the vehicle? Here again, time in inventory matters. The "go away" date for a vehicle depends on the dealer, but you can bet it's tied to a specific days-in-inventory interval, often 45, 60, or 90 days.

FRONT-END GROSS: A FOCUS FOR THE AGES

As Chris and I thought more deeply about the role of time in used vehicles, it became eminently clear that both time and front-end gross profit are deeply connected in the minds of dealers.

In fact, we realized that the interplay between time and

front-end gross profit has led to an industry-wide belief that's been around since the day a dealer sold the first used car—that the time you hold a vehicle equates to the profit potential each vehicle holds.

My dad and I certainly paid super close attention to the time used vehicles spent in inventory at our Cadillac dealership. Like everyone else before us and since, we knew that used vehicles depreciate over time, and as time passes and depreciation occurs, front-end gross profits tend to diminish.

There's also no question that the long-standing belief that time in inventory functions as a suitable measure of a used vehicle's money-making potential became a foundational pillar of the Velocity Method of Management.

The turn-and-earn principles that underlie Velocity are inextricably linked with the idea that the sooner you retail a used vehicle, the more money you make.

But Chris and I noticed a curious disconnect or deception between time and front-end gross profits—specifically, when the relationship between the two *doesn't* seem to matter.

For example, when dealers retail a vehicle and earn a gross profit, they often don't consider how long it took them to make the money or the amount of money they had to invest in the vehicle to make the gross profit.

For example, let's say Dealer A has a $30,000 vehicle that produces a $3,000 front-end gross when the vehicle retails at 60 days in inventory.

Dealer B, meanwhile, has a $20,000 vehicle that produces a $2,000 front-end gross when the vehicle retails at 30 days.

Right off the bat, most dealers would recognize that each dealer's gross profit represents 10 percent of the respective transaction prices.

But let's ask the question: Which dealer is better off from an ROI perspective?

The correct answer is Dealer B. He/she invested less money, and it took half the time to earn the same 10 percent return as Dealer A.

What's more, Dealer B has another 30 days to reallocate the capital to another vehicle and repeat the retail cycle.

While most dealers recognize that Dealer B is doing better from an investment perspective, the recognition doesn't seem to carry over into the day-to-day decisions they make in used vehicles.

When Chris and I arrived at this realization, we had a hold-your-horses moment.

We were struck by the fact that, even as dealers focused on time in inventory and front-end gross profit, they were missing what might be the single most important factor for their ability to drive a net profit from a retail used vehicle sale—the vehicle's actual ROI, not just its front-end gross profit.

That's when Chris and I began connecting a couple of dots and asking some serious questions:

Is time in inventory even a relevant measure of a used vehicle's ROI or net profit potential? And if it isn't, what is?

If dealers are ultrafocused on the connection between time in inventory and front-end gross profit with little or no regard for a used vehicle's ROI, could this mindset be making the Cost to Market appreciation problem we'd discovered even worse?

The questions demanded additional investigation and research.

Chris and his data scientist team went back to the vAuto archive of dealer inventory and transaction data.

We weren't exactly sure what we'd find, but we were committed to answering the questions and potentially satisfying our curiosity.

CHAPTER 9

A HOLE IN THE USED CAR UNIVERSE

There's a long list of what have come to be considered "accidental discoveries."

There's the microwave, which American engineer Percy Spencer is credited with discovering while working with a radar in a laboratory. He noticed that microwaves from the radar melted a chocolate bar in his pocket—an accident that led to the invention of a kitchen appliance most of us would have trouble living without.

There's insulin. The story behind insulin starts with two European doctors who, in 1889, were working to understand the role that the pancreas plays in digestion. They removed the pancreas from a dog as part of their experiment and noticed flies had become attracted to its urine, due to higher levels of sugar. About 30 years later, two Canadian researchers built on this happy accident. They identified that the pancreas produced insulin to regulate glucose levels in humans—a finding that led to a Nobel Prize and commercial availability of insulin to help people with diabetes.

There's Viagra. In the late 1980s and early 1990s, the drug company Pfizer had introduced sildenafil as a high blood pressure medication. Clinical trials showed that the drug wasn't effective for that purpose. But male clinical trial patients noticed a different side effect and reportedly didn't want to give unused meds back to researchers after the trial. The Food and Drug Administration approved Viagra in 1998, and the "little blue pill" has been with us ever since.

In each of these cases and a host of others, someone was curious about, looking for, or trying to prove something but wound up discovering something else.

That's exactly what happened to vAuto's Chris Stutsman and me.

In 2017, we started out to gain a better explanation and understanding of the reasons behind the dramatic and sudden rise of Cost to Market percentages.

Along the way, we realized and recognized the New Math of Used Vehicles and the necessity for dealers to balance the New Math Equation if they expected to improve the net profitability of their used vehicle departments.

Next, we began asking some deep questions about the role of time itself in used vehicles, as well as whether a focus on front-end gross profit and the lack of attention to ROI might be making it more difficult for dealers to make money in their used vehicle departments.

But we did not expect to discover what I have since come to call a "hole in the used car universe."

TWO TIME-RELATED PROBLEMS IN USED VEHICLE MANAGEMENT

As Chris and I returned to the vAuto inventory data and research, we decided that we had to essentially shed what we thought we knew about the used car business.

We singled out some specific front-end gross- and time-based beliefs and best practices in used vehicle management. We began testing them against the inventory and transaction data in vAuto's archive.

We wanted to know whether the time a dealer holds a vehicle in inventory truly serves as an indicator of a used vehicle's ROI, or net profit potential.

We tested the long-standing premise that "fresh cars" deliver the best grosses, and therefore represent the best money-making opportunities in any used car business.

We also wanted to know if we could find any correlation between the time a dealer holds a vehicle in inventory and the front-end gross profit it generates with the net profit or ROI a used vehicle transaction brings to the bottom line.

We also asked ourselves a left-field question: If we don't find any relevance or utility between time, front-end grosses, and ROI, what factors might be better indicators or measures?

From a data crunching and research perspective, we'd just outlined a tall order.

That's when Chris pulled his data scientist hat on a little tighter.

From the inventory and transaction data from vAuto, he pulled 10 years' worth of vehicles and deals, which numbered in the millions.

He diced, sliced, and tested the data for several months. Ultimately, he came back with a couple of key conclusions:

First, while time in inventory appeared to track closely with front-end gross profits, it didn't work all that well as an indicator of a vehicle's net profit or ROI potential.

Chris examined hundreds of transactions that involved "fresh" cars. Indeed, the front-end gross profits on these vehicles tended to be higher than other vehicles in inventories.

But we also found a sizable number of deals involving "fresh units" that did not contribute to ROI or appear to make a positive net profit contribution.

Second, Chris found that while vehicles that had been in dealer inventories for some time tended to bear smaller front-end gross profits when they retailed, there were plenty of deals that didn't fit this mold.

In fact, Chris found that with some aged vehicles, a smaller front-end gross profit produced a satisfying, if not significant, ROI or net profit for the used vehicle department.

This insight led to a third takeaway: that a vehicle's front-end gross profit is a flawed indicator or measure of its net profit or ROI contribution—a gross deception.

Finally, Chris found that while time in inventory or front-end gross profits weren't reliable indicators or measures of a used vehicle's ROI or net profit potential, there were a couple of other variables that showed promise.

Namely, Chris began to understand that a vehicle's Cost to Market, Market Days Supply, and Retail Sales Volumes actually *did* serve as reliable predictors of its ROI or net profit potential. This was a pivotal and profound moment for both of us.

I asked Chris: "Did we just prove that days in inventory, or Calendar Time, isn't a relevant or reliable yardstick for dealers to manage a used vehicle to its optimal net profit and ROI potential?"

"That's what it looks like, Dale," Chris replied.

I knew, at that moment, that Chris and I had discovered the equivalent of a hole in the used car universe, that two pre-eminent areas of focus—a vehicle's days or time in inventory (Calendar Time) and its front-end gross profit potential—had little, if any, bearing or relevance on a vehicle's ROI or net profit potential.

These were two glaring examples of gross deception.

Both of us were a little taken aback by what we'd found. After all, we'd built the vAuto software and the Velocity Method of Management around the concept that time in inventory really matters.

We were amazed that our discovery suggested that managing a used vehicle's time in inventory to maximize front-end gross profit—a principle that had served the industry for nearly 100 years—amounted to a faulty premise.

If we were correct, how was it even possible that in all those years, no one had figured out that while Calendar Time might have been directionally correct, it wasn't a reliable gauge of a given used vehicle's ROI or money-making potential?

We arrived at an answer that made perfect sense: For many years, dealers made a sufficient amount of money in used vehicles that they didn't have a cause or a reason to question whether the foundation on which their management decisions stood was truly correct. It worked. End of story.

But the sharp decline in used vehicle net profits that NADA reported for 2017 changed all that.

In a way, the precipitous drop of net profitability served as a fog lifter.

It gave Chris and me a clearer view. It allowed us to poke and prod the roots of the used car business itself.

It allowed us the opportunity to take a more critical, deeper look at inventory and transaction data, and to ask the questions that previously hadn't been worth asking.

It was also around this time that Chris and I began to go bananas.

CHAPTER 10

STRANGE BEDFELLOWS: BANANAS AND USED VEHICLES

When vAuto's Chris Stutsman and I realized that our findings would effectively upend the long-standing beliefs and best practices about the role of time in used vehicles, we knew we'd need a way to help illustrate why days in inventory, or Calendar Time, isn't a useful measure of a used vehicle's ROI or money-making potential.

We landed on bananas and the concept of ripeness.

We can all recognize the ripeness of a banana, and we also understand that bananas go through stages or ripeness over time.

On Day 1, bananas are green, full of potential, with lots of time ahead.

After a few days pass, you have a bright yellow, perfectly ripe banana.

We know the banana's in its prime, and we also know it won't stay like this forever.

That's because, after a few more days pass, the banana starts showing brown spots and bruises.

The banana's no longer as appealing to look at, and if you peel one and eat it, the mushier, softer texture isn't as satisfying.

If you were selling this banana, you'd have to give it a heavy discount, because its condition is only going to get worse.

A few more days pass, and you've got a gooey, rotten banana.

It's arrived at the stage where, if you don't throw it out or use it for baking, you'll have a cloud of fruit flies in your kitchen, if you don't already.

In this way, bananas are a lot like used vehicles. Time diminishes their respective profit potential and value.

But Chris and I also recognized that bananas and used vehicles have some distinct differences.

For one, while bananas tend to age at the same rate, time affects different used vehicles at different rates.

We made this conclusion after the inventory data showed us that some "fresh" cars weren't as ROI productive as their days in inventory, or Calendar Time, might have you believe.

Similarly, we found that with some aged cars, the ROI and net profit potential hadn't run out when they retailed.

If we had two different used vehicles, each might start out as green bananas on Day 1.

By Day 15, the used vehicles might still share the same level of ripeness. Both are bright yellow bananas, ostensibly at their peak ROI and net profit potential.

But by Day 30, one of the vehicles could still be a bright yellow banana, while the other has turned brown and bruised.

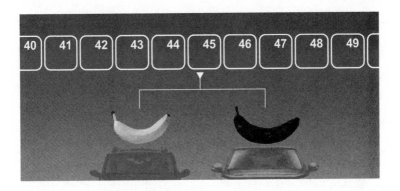

By Day 45, the conditions that allowed one of the vehicles to remain a bright yellow banana might still hold, while the other has turned gooey and rotten. The graphic illustrates this reality.

If we asked ourselves what days in inventory, or Calendar Time, told us about the ROI or net profit potential of the vehicles at each time interval, the answer would be very little, if anything.

Sometimes a vehicle's Calendar Time correlates with its ROI or net profit potential. Other times, it doesn't.

Chris and I also recognized that dealers don't always work with green bananas on Day 1.

That's because dealers take in used vehicles at varying stages of their ripeness or ROI potential.

Some are green. Some are yellow. Some are brown and bruised.

Dealers might even be taking home a gooey rotten banana

on Day 1. Maybe it happened by accident, or maybe it was on purpose. Maybe the dealer chose to buy a rotten banana to close another deal.

Whatever the case, if you look at the cross-section of "fresh" cars on the day they arrive at a dealership, the days in inventory, or Calendar Time, doesn't say much, if anything, about their ROI and net profit potential.

The same is true, though perhaps to a lesser degree, for aged vehicles. Sometimes their time in inventory correlates to ROI and net profit potential; other times it doesn't.

When I share the banana analogy with dealers, it often feels familiar.

It speaks to the situations they see in their stores where certain vehicles, despite being "fresh," simply don't deliver the front-end gross they expect.

Dealers can also relate to the times when they finally retail an aged unit and it produces more front-end gross than anyone expected, given the time in inventory.

As Chris and I reflected on the differences between bananas and used vehicles, we began to question if there would be a way that used vehicles could be more like bananas.

We thought: Wouldn't it be cool if we could develop a color-coding system that would give dealers an instant read on a vehicle's ROI or net profit potential? Wouldn't it be extremely useful for dealers to understand this critical money-making aspect of a used vehicle on Day 1, and every day in inventory afterward?

That's the working framework and vision that Chris took back to his team of data scientists.

The good news? We discovered a way to render a used vehicle's ROI and net profit potential with a predictive, color-coded system.

Even better, it works.

Now let's have a look at how and why it works.

CHAPTER 11

A NEW ALGORITHM AND A HOLY S**T MOMENT

I t was an exhilarating idea—that maybe, just maybe, we might find a way for dealers to know, with reliable certainty, the ROI or net profit potential of every used vehicle. We were excited to focus our attention and time on figuring out how we could make identifying used vehicle retail and ROI prospects as easy as looking at a banana.

But it wasn't long after we set out along this road that we encountered a profound realization—that we essentially had to build the road if we were going to be successful.

The realization came shortly after we began focusing on how a vehicle's Cost to Market, Market Days Supply, and Retail Sales Volumes—the variables that Chris and team had identified as potential predictors of ROI and net profit—could be conjoined to give us accurate and reliable predictions.

Here's an example: If you gave equal weight to each of the

variables, one of them, Cost to Market, tended to wash out the effects of the others.

The washout made perfect sense. If you acquire a used vehicle for $1,000 and know that its prevailing retail asking price runs close to $10,000, you've got a unit with a 10 percent Cost to Market percentage.

The vehicle didn't require much for the initial investment, and its spread between your cost and its likely retail selling price would suggest that you'd make a substantial ROI and net profit contribution, even if the vehicle took awhile to retail.

Similarly, Chris and team noted that the Cost to Market percentages on more expensive vehicles tended to run higher in relation to their retail asking prices than less expensive inventory.

This takeaway stood to reason, given that more expensive vehicles are typically less than three years old. Demand among dealers and consumers is high for these vehicles, a fact of life that results in higher acquisition costs, and therefore higher Cost to Market percentages, to own them compared to other vehicles.

I distinctly remember wondering, as Chris and his team were poking and prodding the data, if we'd ever find an answer.

But one day my phone rang. It was Chris.

"Dale, I think we've got it," Chris told me. "We've figured out a way to adjust the weightings of the three variables on an individual vehicle basis. By doing that, we can account for the characteristics that matter for a specific vehicle but might matter less for the next one. In the end, we've built an algorithm that can predict a vehicle's ROI and net profit potential."

I was stoked. Then, I was worried.

"Are you sure?" I asked Chris.

"110 percent positive, Dale," he said. "We can rerun the numbers if you'd like to make absolutely certain."

No, I told Chris. We didn't need to go back and redo the numbers.

We needed to go forward. We needed to test the algorithm in the real world—against the current vehicles in vAuto dealer inventories, not just the historical cars and transactions that vAuto kept in its archive.

My request meant a few more months of data crunching, and some restless nights for me.

I managed to get myself to sleep knowing that Chris and team were headed in the right direction.

They were looking to prove, beyond any doubt, that there is a better way than relying on days in inventory and front-end gross profits to discern a used vehicle's ROI or net profit potential.

They had also built an algorithm that accounted for something that dealers had long overlooked—that *when* you earn the front-end gross profit can, in some cases, matter as much, if not more, than the actual amount you make, if your primary goal is maximizing the net profit of your used vehicle department.

I remember falling asleep one night thinking: If the algorithm doesn't work and we can't make identifying a vehicle's ROI and net profit potential as easy as knowing when a banana is ripe or rotten, then at least we can help dealers focus on making sure the net profit they make in used vehicles is a positive number.

AN ALGORITHM-DRIVEN HOLYS**T MOMENT

I was excited when Chris shared the news that he and his data scientists had made a positive correlation between the properly weighted combination of a vehicle's Cost to Market, Market Days Supply, and Retail Sales Volume, and the unit's ROI and money-making potential.

From what they were telling me, they'd cracked the ROI nut. They'd built an accurate, reliable algorithm that could predict a used vehicle's ROI or money-making potential.

But I was concerned that all of their work was based on historical data—the decade's worth of vehicles and transactions housed in vAuto's data archive.

I was worried that there might be some market condition or unknown nuance that might make this trove of historical data irrelevant for today's market.

That's why I asked Chris and his team to see how the new algorithm worked when it was applied to the vehicles vAuto dealers had in their inventories right now.

I had to know if this new algorithm held up to current market conditions.

To do this work, Chris and his team developed a 12-point scoring system and precious metal designations (Platinum, Gold, Silver, and Bronze) to classify and represent each vehicle's ROI or money-making potential. The scores are derived from the weighted combination of variables built into the algorithm.

For example, a vehicle that you own right (as evidenced by a low Cost to Market percentage), that the market loves (as evidenced by a low Market Days Supply), and that sells well (as evidenced by high Retail Sales Volume) would receive an Investment Score between 10 and 12. The system would designate the vehicle as Platinum.

Conversely, a vehicle that you don't own right (as evidenced by a high Cost to Market percentage), that the market doesn't love (as evidenced by a high Market Days Supply), and that sells poorly (as evidenced by low Retail Sales Volume) would receive an Investment Score between 1 and 3. The system would designate this vehicle as Bronze.

Chris and his team applied the algorithm and scoring system to more than one million vehicles in dealer inventories. They scored every vehicle every day, and then rescored them every night.

They also tracked when each vehicle transacted and, using a combination of the vehicle's market-clearing Price to Market percentage and transaction data, produced an estimated transaction price for every vehicle.

We embarked on this months-long data-crunching experiment with the hope that we could apply our new algorithm and Investment Score to vehicles today and that it would actually work as an accurate predictor of a used vehicle's ROI or net profit potential.

Well, it did. We were very excited. We had proven our premise. We knew we had something big to offer the industry.

Around that time, I was curious to see how well dealer inventories actually scored, in terms of their investment values, when we applied the algorithm to the vehicles they currently had in stock.

Chris and his team dutifully went back to work and brought back more than I'd asked for.

They produced a national composite of the Investment Scores and precious metal classifications for all of the vehicles in vAuto dealer inventories in the United States.

To be honest, I wasn't sure what I'd find when I asked Chris and his team for a national view of inventory investment values.

But when I saw the composite, it was like I got hit by a truck. It was another "holy s**t" moment of discovery.

The composite essentially showed that every vAuto dealer in the country was making suboptimal and often irrational decisions about their used vehicle investments.

Every single dealer's inventory was inverted from an investment value perspective.

Dealers were pricing their most ROI- and profit-productive vehicles, the Platinum cars, to sell fast. Too fast, actually, given their appeal to the market.

And, at the same time, they were pricing their least ROI- and profit-productive Bronze vehicles the most proudly—too proudly, in fact, when you consider these vehicles were really brown, bruised, and rotten bananas.

At first, I was convinced the composite was incorrect.

I've been around the car business a long time. It's a rare thing when you get two or more dealers to agree on much of anything.

It seemed impossible and flat-out wrong that 100 percent of dealers would be doing the exact same thing, much less something as irrational and suboptimal as the composite showed.

I simply couldn't believe that the near-uniform investment management inversion in dealer inventories was anything but a mistake in the math.

I asked Chris to confirm that the composite was correct. He and his team went back and analyzed the numbers even more closely.

"The composite's correct, Dale," Chris told me. "The numbers are good. It sure looks like there's an investment value problem out there."

Well, there you have it, I thought. The composite is so disturbing and so telling that it merits more scrutiny.

It deserves its own chapter, and it's up next.

CHAPTER 12

A COMPOSITE OF INVESTMENT DISTRESS AND INDIFFERENCE

W hen vAuto's Chris Stutsman showed me the national composite of dealer inventories in the United States as measured by investment value, we probably spent an hour on a "what's wrong with this picture?" discussion.

We marveled at all the ways the influence of Calendar Time and a focus on front-end gross profits led dealers to make decisions that, from an investment perspective, were irrational and counterproductive to their ultimate mission and purpose in used vehicles—to maximize net profit.

It blew me away that the investment inversion Chris and team had discovered proved to be prevalent in every dealer's inventory.

NATIONAL COMPOSITE

Time	% Vehicles	Avg. Price to Market	Avg. Cost to Market	Avg. Days Supply	Avg. Age
Platinum	19%	96.40%	81.40%	48	35
Gold	29%	97.40%	88.0%	68	39
Silver	25%	99.00%	93.50%	70	47
Bronze	28%	101.00%	100.40%	74	81

The more I stared at the composite, and its proof of widespread gross deception, the more I realized that vAuto had another opportunity to change the industry for the better.

I understood that if every dealer suffered from the investment inversion problem, it suggested that there was a big opportunity to help dealers find a better way to manage their used vehicle investments to yield richer ROI and healthier net profits.

I also gained confidence in the opportunity as I began showing dealers an investment value composite of their own inventories. The reactions followed a similar pattern: from shocked and stunned to hungry and motivated for a better way.

This is the backdrop for the National Composite chart that we'll now dissect in this chapter. I've combined the critical takeaways into two buckets.

BUCKET I: A PRICING PROBLEM

When I share the composite with dealers, I'll ask: "What's the first problem you see?"

I'd estimate that roughly 75 percent of dealers land on the same issue I found to be most glaring and disturbing on the composite—the way dealers are pricing their Bronze and Platinum vehicles.

Look at the Bronze vehicles. Collectively, the average Price to Market percentage for Bronze vehicles is 101 percent. The average means that dealers are pricing their Bronze vehicles—the ones that represent the least in terms of ROI and net profit potential—the most proudly out of all the vehicles in their inventories.

Let's go a little further: Take note of the average days in inventory of the Bronze vehicles, which is 81 days. That's the highest average days in inventory among all the vehicle groupings.

I'll suggest to dealers that a primary reason their Bronze vehicles aren't selling is because they're priced too high. Most agree.

Look at the Platinum vehicles. The composite shows that the Price to Market percentage for Platinum vehicles is 96.4 percent. The average means that dealers are pricing their Platinum vehicles—the ones that represent the greatest ROI and net profit potential, commanding the highest appeal in the market—the least proudly of all their vehicles.

Now note the average days in inventory for Platinum vehicles. It's 35 days.

I'll suggest to dealers that a primary reason their Platinum vehicles are selling the fastest is because dealers are giving them away and leaving money on the table.

When I walk through the pricing problem the composite reveals with dealers, most immediately recognize that they would make more money if they did two things—lower the price of their Bronze vehicles to sell them faster, and raise the prices of their Platinum vehicles to make more gross profit on the vehicles that deserve it.

For some dealers, the repricing can bring short-term financial pain. The degree of pain depends on the number of Bronze and Silver vehicles in their inventories that, when priced correctly, will result in retail losses.

But these losses are often short lived and far less than the ongoing financial pain dealers are enduring in their used vehicle departments that results from irrational pricing of a sizable share of their used vehicles.

In fact, the prevalence of the pricing problem suggests it's almost like a blind spot on a car—you can't and won't see what's in your way unless you get out of the car and look.

These days, when dealers complain that they aren't making enough or they're losing money in used vehicles, I'll show them a composite of their own inventories.

It's often a moment that brings recognition that, if they want to correct the net profit problem in their used vehicle department, they've got some work to do.

BUCKET 2: INVENTORY INVESTMENT DISTRIBUTION

When dealers see the inventory investment composite, they're also quick to note the distribution of Platinum, Gold, Silver, and Bronze vehicles in their inventories.

Specifically, they'll note that they have a lot more Bronze (28 percent) than Platinum (19 percent) vehicles.

Some go a step further.

They'll note that if you combine the Bronze (28 percent) and Silver (25 percent) vehicles, you've got more than half of the typical dealer's inventory—53 percent, to be precise—tied up in the lowest-performing investments.

Next, the dealers will think they're doing something wrong. That the prevalence of Bronze and Silver vehicles amounts to a big mistake—and that they should stock more Platinum vehicles.

I try to calm the concern. The fact that 53 percent of a dealer's inventory consists of Bronze and Silver vehicles *might* be a mistake from a management perspective.

But it might not be, either.

My view is that the shares of Bronze and Silver vehicles in dealer inventories are signs of the harsh realities of today's market.

It's evidence of the faster appreciation of Cost to Market percentages and the rise of the New Math in Used Vehicles.

It reflects the fact that, in today's market, there are just some vehicles where, regardless of what Calendar Time tells you, represent a less-than-ideal investment that should be managed as such.

I'll also discuss the dealers' immediate reaction about the

share of Platinum cars in their inventories—that they should get to work and focus on stocking more of them.

But here's the thing. Where will a dealer consistently find enough Platinum vehicles to make it a viable retailing strategy?

As a rule, Platinum vehicles have low Market Days Supply, favorable Cost to Market percentages, and high Retail Sales Volumes.

In plain terms, they're the best of the best—highly appealing vehicles to dealers and customers alike, which means, by their nature, Platinum vehicles are more scarce to find and stock.

You might be able to find a Platinum vehicle at an auction, but it's probably a rare bird.

Similarly, in today's era of vehicle affordability challenges, which have owners keeping their cars longer and leasing, you're less likely to have as many trade-ins, which is the most likely source for Platinum vehicles.

The bottom line on the inventory investment distribution is this: The respective shares of Platinum, Gold, Silver, and Bronze vehicles are less important than what you do to manage the vehicles to optimize their respective investment values.

The composite suggests an immediate opportunity: Dealers could take their Bronze and Silver vehicles—the 53 percent of their inventories that represents distressed and least-favorable investments—and reprice them more rationally compared to competing vehicles in the market.

What do you think would happen if a dealer did this—reprice every Bronze and Silver vehicle based on its investment value—tomorrow?

The answer is that the dealer would see an instant spike in volume, albeit with less front-end gross profit than most dealers would like. Meanwhile, the F&I and Service departments would be stoked with the additional business.

But the diminished front-end gross would be temporary, if and only if dealers viewed this dispatching of their most distressed used vehicle investments for what it is—a clearing of the table that makes way for more efficient, fast treatment of Bronze and Silver vehicles from this day forward.

The composite also suggests another opportunity—one that recognizes time in inventory only matters when it relates to a vehicle's individual investment value.

Consider the average age of Bronze and Platinum vehicles on the composite.

It shows 81 days for Bronze vehicles and 35 days for Platinum vehicles.

Now imagine for a moment what would happen if you flipped those numbers? If you sold all of your Bronze vehicles in 35 days, instead of 81, and you sold all of your Platinum vehicles within 80 days, instead of 35?

Most dealers recognize the right answer—they'd be making more front-end gross profit and seeing healthier ROI and net profit outcomes.

Such opportunities-in-waiting beg some critical questions: Why aren't dealers treating their Bronze and Platinum vehicles this way already? What's stopping them from enjoying the improvement in both gross and net profit that a more investment value–attuned management strategy might deliver?

There are three answers.

First, there's tradition. Dealers have become so accustomed to regarding time in inventory, or Calendar Time, as indicative of a used vehicle's front-end gross profit potential that it's deeply ingrained in how they think about and manage their used vehicle investments.

Second, dealers aren't aware of how their reliance on Calendar Time and front-end gross negatively affect the net profit potential of their used vehicle department. In many ways, the lack of awareness seems to be making the problem of Cost to Market appreciation and losses in net profit even worse in used vehicles.

Third, there's human nature. Like anyone else, dealers and their managers don't like to face financial losses and often actively work to avoid them.

The combination of these factors results in many irrational decisions that diminish the ROI and net profit potential of used vehicle departments.

Let's take a closer look at how these factors currently play out in the day-to-day decisions dealers and managers make about their used vehicle investments.

CHAPTER 13

WHO'S GOING TO JUMP ON THE GRENADE?

When I was a kid, Saturday mornings were the bomb.

My brothers and I would invariably wake up before my parents.

We'd turn on the TV and plant ourselves with pillows on the floor.

Sometimes, all we watched were the black-and-white color test bars from the broadcast stations in Northwest Indiana.

Six a.m. was the witching hour. It's when Looney Tunes and the Road Runner took over.

My brothers and I would watch as much as we could until breakfast. If we were lucky, we might have more cartoon time after breakfast.

But there were some Saturdays when circumstances or the weather made it so I'd be watching TV around 10 or 11 a.m.

At that time, I could switch channels and find war movies

and westerns. If memory serves, Channel 9 carried this programming most regularly.

I liked westerns, but like a lot of other boys in my neighborhood, I really liked war movies.

I suspect it was the combination of combat, guns, bravery, sacrifice, and valor that captivated me.

I was especially moved by the scenes that depicted someone falling on a live hand grenade to protect his fellow soldiers.

As a viewer, you felt sad. The guy, who you'd probably come to know as someone who cared about folks back home and who worried about right and wrong, was suddenly gone.

I'm sure other viewers gained the same solace as me. We knew that the soldier's sacrifice served a greater good. The soldier's final, heroic act also inspired. It fed into our own games of "war" in the neighborhood, in which someone, sometimes me, would pretend a live grenade just rolled into our foxhole.

I'm reminded of these boyhood memories and movies as I consider the chronic investment inversion problem in dealer inventories across the country.

It's basically a situation where no one wants to jump on the grenade.

No one wants to deal with the poorest-performing investments—the Bronze and Silver cars—that arrive in dealer inventories. Nobody wants to reckon with the fact that these vehicles don't deserve the asking prices and time on the lot that they get.

In some ways, you can't blame anyone for not wanting to deal with the problem of lesser-performing inventory investments.

First, most dealers and used vehicle managers aren't groomed and trained to manage used vehicles as investments. They know the blocking and tackling that's been handed down for generations—that losses are bad, gross profit is good, and the time you hold a vehicle equates to the amount of profit each vehicle holds.

It's a management framework that's worked for a long time.

But, as I've tried to point out throughout this book, it's a framework that has significant flaws, and one that enhances the effects of market efficiency and margin compression.

Second, there's human nature and two natural tendencies— to avoid pain and loss, and to take the easy road when you can.

I can't think of anyone I know who wakes up in the morning and seeks out pain and loss. Can you?

I suspect the answer is a firm "no."

I'd also submit that the car business is full of people who are especially well wired to avoid pain and loss, particularly when it's financial in nature.

At least part of the reason that Bronze and Silver vehicles are priced too high and often languish too long on dealer lots is because of the financial pain and loss that most dealers and managers would suffer if they reckoned with them in a much more capital-efficient, investment-minded manner.

Who's going to jump on the grenade that represents a retail loss of $1,000 or more on Day 1?

This is why the Bronze and Silver vehicles get kicked down the road. No one has an incentive to deal with them in the manner their respective ROI and net profit potential would warrant.

There's also our predilection for taking the easy road if we can.

It's this aspect of human nature that I believe accounts for the way dealers and managers handle their Platinum investments.

As we discussed in the last chapter, the composite revealed that dealers are pricing Platinum vehicles more aggressively than they should, given their investment status, and leaving gross profit on the table as a result.

You have to ask: If everyone's so keenly focused on front-end gross profit, why aren't they going for gross on the vehicles, specifically the Platinum and Gold cars, that deserve the shot to make gross?

The answer is tied to the marching orders that used vehicle managers often get from their dealers and, in some cases, their Performance Managers.

Dealers will constantly push their managers to increase their sales volumes. Similarly, Performance Managers will coach the managers to look for ways to increase inventory turns.

But here's the rub for the men and women in the manager's hot seat: Half of their inventory is tied up in Bronze and Silver vehicles that aren't priced rationally and, as a result, aren't well positioned for a retail sale.

So where do the managers go to satisfy the dealer's desire for more volume and the Performance Manager's press for inventory turns?

They take the easy way out.

They go to the Platinum and Gold cars—the ones that sell fast because they have relatively low Market Days Supply metrics, high Retail Sales Volumes, and they're priced to move at an average 96 percent Price to Market percentage (Platinum) or 97 percent Price to Market percentage (Gold).

When these vehicles retail, they make a decent gross profit. The managers and sales associates high-five each other on closing a deal that earned a respectable front-end gross profit.

But what they don't realize is that they probably could have made even more money if they'd been more patient and less aggressive with their pricing, given the investment value of the Platinum and Gold vehicles.

Some dealers push back on this point.

They'll argue that if they don't price Platinum vehicles aggressively, they won't show up in searches on classified and other sites and achieve the Vehicle Details Page (VDP) views with buyers.

That's when I ask a key question:

Do you have some vehicles that retail almost as soon as you acquire them?

Most dealers can identify such vehicles, the ones that get inquiries and offers almost as soon as they go up online.

Such vehicles are naturals—units that, because of how well you own them and their appeal in the market, naturally find buyers.

These vehicles are your Platinum vehicles. Their favorable Cost to Market, Market Days Supply, and Retail Sales Volume characteristics make them "naturals" that do not require the same aggressive prices and corresponding VDP views to earn a buyer.

What's more, your sales associates know they can make a good commission on the vehicles, and they're anxious to show them to customers.

My overall point is that, whether it's Platinum, Gold, Bronze, or Silver vehicles, dealers have an opportunity to break the unvirtuous cycle of pricing some vehicles too cheaply and others too expensively, in a way that optimizes each vehicle's ROI and net profit potential.

It starts with a more investment-astute approach to the way dealers acquire inventory.

If dealers really knew what the net profit and ROI potential might be for any used vehicle from the moment they decided to purchase it, it stands to reason that dealers and used vehicle managers would make pricing decisions that better reflected each unit's inherent investment value (or lack thereof).

This belief led vAuto's Chris Stutsman and me to develop a way that dealers could see the key insights they needed in one place, to make more investment-minded acquisition decisions that set the stage for more rational, investment value–based pricing.

CHAPTER 14

A TRIFECTA OF INSIGHTS TO MAKE INVESTMENT-SMART ACQUISITIONS

After vAuto's Chris Stutsman and I analyzed the national composite of dealer inventories, we asked ourselves a key question:

What insights might help dealers avoid making investment-adverse decisions when they're appraising and acquiring inventory?

We knew that part of the answer rested in the investment value algorithm that Chris and team produced.

We believed its 1–12 scoring system and the associated precious metal designations (Platinum, Gold, Silver, and Bronze) would go a long way toward helping dealers know, with unprecedented certainty, the ROI and net profit potential of each used vehicle.

But we also understood a few facts about the way dealers typically acquire used vehicles.

First, we knew that when dealers view an Investment Score composite of their own inventories, they immediately think they have too many Bronze and Silver vehicles and that they should work to get more Platinum and Gold vehicles.

The problem, though, is that Platinum and Gold vehicles simply aren't as plentiful in the market as Bronze and Silver vehicles—a reflection, I think, of a market where there's far greater price awareness, competition, and transparency than ever before.

I'll often ask dealers: Where are you going to find a sufficient supply of vehicles with a low Market Days Supply and high Retail Sales Volumes and buy them on the cheap?

In my view, you might be able to find some Platinum and Gold vehicles at auction, but certainly not enough to follow a strategy where you avoid the Bronze and Silver vehicles.

Similarly, the best source for Platinum and Gold vehicles is typically through trade-ins, but the share of new vehicle deals that include a trade-in has been shrinking, not growing, in recent years.

Second, we understood that, by and large, dealers believe that paying too much for a vehicle is a mistake. I know the feeling. There's nothing worse than bringing home vehicles from an auction or acquiring one through a trade-in and realizing you could have purchased the vehicle for far less money.

But Chris and I also reasoned that there probably were times, especially in today's market, when paying too much for a vehicle might not be a mistake. In fact, it might be completely unavoidable and, depending on the circumstances, the exactly right thing to do.

Third, we also knew that, if you examine vehicles that have been in dealer inventories for 60 days or more, you'll typically see that a majority of these vehicles—sometimes as much as 70 percent—were purchased at auctions.

This percentage has been a consistent talking point for vAuto Performance Managers with dealer clients since we started the company. The long-standing ubiquity of this conversation suggests that, at least when it comes to auction purchases, something seems amiss in the way buyers determine if a vehicle and its purchase price are "right" for a dealer's inventory.

With these facts in mind, Chris and I recognized right away that while the Investment Score we'd developed would most certainly help dealers make more investment-astute decisions to acquire inventory, the score in and of itself wouldn't be enough.

The Investment Score alone, for example, doesn't account for the circumstances and context that surround every potential used vehicle acquisition. While the Investment Score may help you understand a vehicle's ROI and net profit potential, it doesn't tell you if you need a specific car or the degree to which your market likes the car or doesn't.

This thinking led us to develop what we've come to call "The Trifecta," a trio of insights that, historically, dealers don't seem to account for consistently enough, or especially in conjunction with one another, as they acquire used vehicles.

The Trifecta combines the three requisites—the Money, the Market, and the Mix—that we believe will help dealers approach any used vehicle acquisition with a full accounting of its ROI and net profit potential, as well as the circumstances and context that help determine whether a purchase makes good sense for the used vehicle department.

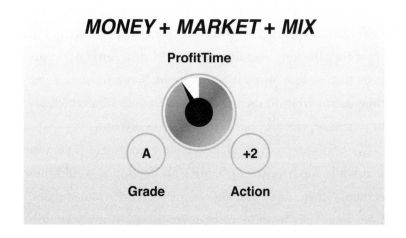

Here's a quick rundown:

1. **THE MONEY:** It's well understood that the money you pay to acquire a vehicle at auction or trade-in sets the stage for its ROI and net profit potential.

> But here's the rub: For decades, dealers haven't really had a way of knowing, from the moment they acquire a vehicle, each vehicle's true investment value.
>
> In fact, the investment inversion we discussed

in previous chapters strikes me as fairly obvious evidence of two possibilities: Either dealers don't know when they've paid too much for a vehicle or purchased a vehicle at the right price, or they don't manage each vehicle to its individual investment value, or lack thereof, once they own it.

Enter the Investment Score. It represents the "money" or the investment value dealers need to know as they acquire inventory at a specific purchase price. It's a metric that sets you up to make better decisions—to price the vehicles with low investment value (your Bronze and Silver units) more aggressively, and to price vehicles with high investment value (your Platinum and Gold units) accordingly.

As one dealer put it, "The Investment Score helps keeps us honest with ourselves about the value a vehicle represents, not what we *think* it represents."

2. **THE MARKET:** It's one thing for a dealer or used vehicle manager to think a used vehicle will be a winner in their local market. It's quite another thing to have the certainty that, in fact, your market really wants the car.

After testing different scenarios and indicators, Chris and I realized that the best available assessment of the current market's interest in a vehicle had already been built. It's the Letter Grade that vAuto's Provisioning module assigns to individual vehicles.

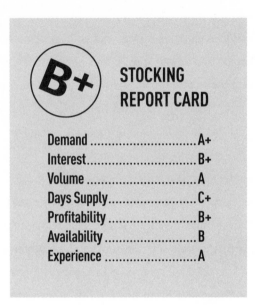

The Letter Grade in the Stocking Report Card results from an algorithm that grades seven different attributes for each vehicle. In the Provisioning module, dealers apply their own weightings to the individual factors to influence the overall Letter Grade. For example, a dealer who prefers to acquire inventory that's familiar and frequently sold could apply a greater weight to "Experience."

For The Trifecta, the Demand and Interest factors offer the most relevant reads on a market's current interest in a specific vehicle. The data comes from Autotrader.com—the number of times online shoppers search for a vehicle (Demand) and the number of times they take a closer look by clicking a Vehicle Details Page (Interest).

> With the Letter Grade in hand, dealers have
> a bead on how easy or difficult it will be to retail a
> specific vehicle—an insight that should not be over-
> looked as dealers aim to make more investment-
> smart inventory acquisitions.

3. **THE MIX:** It'd be an eye-opener, I think, for dealers to know two things about their current acquisition process:

> How many thousands, maybe hundreds of thousands,
> of dollars have you lost in opportunity costs when buy-
> ers walk away from vehicles you really need?
>
> How many thousands, maybe hundreds of thou-
> sands, of dollars have you lost when buyers acquire
> vehicles you really don't need?
>
> I know. I'm being a bit extreme by raising questions
> that can't really be answered.
>
> But I think we can all agree that when someone
> says, "Go get some cars" or a buyer is frustrated that
> they might come home empty-handed from an auction,
> the finer point of whether you really need the vehicle
> gets lost more times than it gets seriously considered.
>
> The Trifecta's Strategy Action brings the point of
> "need" front and center with every potential acquisi-
> tion. The Strategy Action draws from your preferred
> mix of vehicle types (e.g., sub-compacts, SUVs, etc.)
> and retail price points (e.g., $0-$9,999, $10,000-
> $14,999, etc.) for your local market. The Strategy

> Action's + or – designations give you guidance to know
> whether your inventory is long or short with a specific
> vehicle—an insight that's particularly useful when
> you're wondering whether it's best to step up or step
> away from a car.

In some ways, the elements included in The Trifecta represent what the best-of-the-best dealers and used vehicle managers contemplate and sometimes calculate every time they approach and appraise a potential auction or trade-in vehicle.

But I would submit that managers take the holistic view of the circumstances that should be considered to ensure every used vehicle makes sound investment sense less frequently than they could or should at most dealerships.

My dad still ribs me for the time I absolutely blew the purchase of a used 1990 Cadillac Allanté convertible.

I thought it was worth every bit of the $26,000 I paid a buyer for it in early spring of 1991. We were stocking up on convertibles in anticipation of Chicago-area buyers turning their attention to summer.

I liked this car because, while we had other convertibles, we didn't have an Allanté. It was a good-looking car with low miles.

We took a big loss on the car when we finally wholesaled it the following October.

Looking back, if I had The Trifecta in front of me, I would have seen that it was a Bronze vehicle (the purchase price probably should have been south of $20,000), the Letter Grade would have been a D or F (no one in the market really wanted the car, as I learned months later), and the Strategy Action would have been 0, given the other convertibles we already owned.

But this experience will happen far less frequently, I believe, when dealers, managers, appraisers, and buyers consistently use The Trifecta to make holistic, investment-smart used vehicle acquisitions in the context of their market and inventories.

As we'll see in upcoming chapters, The Trifecta fuels a positive outcome for dealers who diligently use it. The composition of their inventory investment values improves. They bring in more Platinum and Gold cars, and they manage the Bronze and Silver vehicles with the greater dispatch and urgency that their lower investment values warrant.

For now, let's take a look at how The Trifecta can help dealers better understand when "paying too much" for a vehicle might be, or might not be, a bad decision given a vehicle's investment value and the other circumstances that surround any used vehicle acquisition decision.

THREE SCENARIOS OF THE TRIFECTA IN ACTION

I've created three hypothetical scenarios to illustrate how The Trifecta can make a big difference in consistently making more holistic and investment-sound acquisition decisions.

The scenarios all involve the same vehicle—a 2014 Chevrolet Malibu—and reflect distinct circumstances that are common for dealers and used vehicle managers every day.

Scenario 1

Let's imagine you're at an auction, in the lane or online. If you want this Malibu, you'll have to pay too much money, which results in an Investment Score of 3 and a Bronze vehicle.

If that's all you know, it might make sense to buy the car, or it might not. The point is that you don't truly know anything more than that if you purchase the car, you'll want to retail it quickly, given its lower investment value.

The key question: *Should* you purchase the vehicle?

You can only arrive at a solid answer to the question by examining the circumstances of your current market and inventory.

From a market perspective, the vehicle is a B+. That's good. The market likes the car.

From an inventory mix perspective, the Strategy Action says you need six cars like this Malibu.

My take on this scenario is that you will be losing retail sales if you *don't* acquire the car, even though you could argue you'd be paying too much.

I would also add that if you buy this Malibu, you'll need to understand that, due to its Bronze status, it's basically a rotten banana. It has a short retail shelf life.

To optimize the vehicle's ROI and net profit potential, you'll want to put it first in line in your reconditioning process and make sure it's priced to sell from Day 1.

Scenario 2

In Scenario 2, we have the same Malibu, for the same amount of money at auction. It's also a Bronze vehicle, with the same Investment Score, a 3.

But other circumstances have changed.

First, the market's not too fond of the car. It's a C-.

Second, you've got nine too many vehicles like the Malibu in your inventory already.

The key question remains: *Should* you buy this car?

If I were a dealer or used vehicle manager, I'd argue that it doesn't make any sense to bring this Malibu into your inventory at the current price. In my book, you should pass on this vehicle and find another one that makes more investment sense.

The point of Scenario 2, of course, is that the circumstances around a vehicle purchase matter more than the vehicle or the purchase price. In this example, the same car, for the same money, made sense in Scenario 1, when you needed the vehicle.

Here, it doesn't make any sense at all—a fact you probably wouldn't know without The Trifecta and the acquisition guidance it offers.

Scenario 3

For Scenario 3, let's imagine that we're not at an auction. We're working a deal.

The customer is holding firm on the amount they want for their trade-in. It's pretty clear—if you want the car, you've got to step up and accept the fact that it's a Silver vehicle, with an Investment Score of 5.

The key question: *Should* you purchase the vehicle?

The market doesn't seem too thrilled about the car; it's a C-.

Your inventory doesn't really need the vehicle, either. The Strategy Action says you've got one too many vehicles like it already in stock.

This scenario paints a less-clear situation than the other two scenarios. It's not a slam-dunk decision one way or the other.

It's a situation where you, as the dealer or used vehicle manager, would need to make the call and accept the consequences that follow. You may have a new vehicle customer who walks, or you've got a Silver investment that's now yours to manage, even though you don't really need it.

My goal in sharing these scenarios is to underscore what The Trifecta is and what it isn't.

The Trifecta is what I consider to be the industry's best guide to ensure that every used vehicle purchase decision accounts for the investment value of the vehicle and the circumstances that determine whether buying the vehicle or walking away from it makes sound investment sense.

The Trifecta helps you get past the idea that paying too much for a vehicle is always a bad idea. As we've seen across the scenarios, sometimes paying too much is a good decision.

The Trifecta also helps you understand what you need to do with the vehicle once you own it. If you pay too much and you don't really need the vehicle, the subsequent steps you take should reflect the fact that you're holding a riskier investment with less retail shelf life.

Conversely, if The Trifecta shows you've got a great car—a Platinum or Gold unit—and you could use it, you don't need quite as much urgency as you do if you bring home a lesser-grade investment.

The Trifecta is *not* designed to make the acquisition decision for you. It gives you the contextual information you need to consider all the circumstances that determine if an investment in a used vehicle is a good decision—or at least one that's made for the right reasons.

Ultimately, though, the decision itself belongs to you, or the person on your team who's responsible for acquiring used vehicle inventory and investing the dealer's money the most efficiently to maximize each vehicle's net profit and ROI potential.

In chapter 21, we'll see how The Trifecta makes infinite sense when it's applied with diligence and intent to make better investment decisions.

But first, let's take a closer look at how we arrived at a name for the system that combines the Investment Score, precious metal designations, and The Trifecta to give dealers unprecedented clarity into a new way of managing their used vehicle investments.

CHAPTER 15

THE MAKINGS OF THE PROFITTIME MONIKER

A round the middle of 2018, vAuto's Chris Stutsman and I faced another hurdle.

We'd discovered the New Math of Used Vehicles.

We'd developed a way to balance the New Math equation.

We'd created the industry's first-ever Investment Score to help dealers know, with certainty, the ROI and net profit potential inherent in every vehicle.

We'd created The Trifecta, a trio of insights that helps dealers ensure that every used vehicle acquisition includes an accounting of the vehicle's investment value and the factors that determine whether purchasing the car makes sound investment sense.

But we needed a name for our new investment value metric and methodology.

That's when I called Tom Barg, the cofounder of Keys and Kites, a Chicago-based agency that specializes in helping businesses create go-to-market messaging for new brands, companies, and products.

Tom is another one of those people I keep in the circle of advisors and confidantes I mentioned in chapter 3.

I've known Tom for close to 15 years, and he was one of the creative minds behind vAuto's initial branding and marketing efforts.

In addition to being a bright, nice guy who loves family, dogs, and music as much as me, Tom possesses the rare ability to take abstract concepts and turn them into something simple, smart, and often profound.

Through his work with vAuto, Tom also knows a bit about the car business and the dealers who make it hum.

I thought: If there's one guy who can take the jumble of things Chris and I have been developing and help us effectively define and bring it to life as a brand and product, it will be Tom.

Chris and I explained the work we'd been doing to create the Investment Score. We shared our discovery that the industry's emphasis on Calendar Time, or time in inventory, and front-end gross profit as measurements of a used vehicle's investment value were flawed and needed to be fixed.

Tom went to work.

"The whole concept struck me as an answer to a problem that required a rethinking of time, not an ignoring of time," he says. "We realized that time on the lot as measured in days, and turn as measured in days, were no longer fine-tuned enough for dealers.

"But we also knew that time is still passing on these investments, and their time as investments is running out. The new idea is that time needs to matter per investment, and every investment clock runs differently.

"It's a flowing of time that's not measured with a clock or a calendar," Tom says. "But it's time measured by the profit potential that exists in a car. It's ProfitTime."

I loved the name the first time Tom shared it.

ProfitTime captured the essence of the difficulties dealers have encountered by considering Calendar Time to be a relevant measure of used vehicle profitability.

ProfitTime introduced an alternate or different dimension of time altogether—exactly what dealers would need to understand the profound nature of this philosophical shift away from Calendar Time.

ProfitTime also gave Tom the inspiration for the clock-based image that holds the Investment Score.

I've always been curious about how Tom comes up with stuff, and I figured he wouldn't mind if I inquired.

TOM AND HIS DOG.

I asked him for a little more background on the process he used to go from a blank sheet of paper to ProfitTime and its clock-based imagery that, to me, make such perfect and easily understandable sense.

"A lot of the work was an attempt to answer the question, 'What kind of metaphor could work in both ways—one that could unify the Investment Score and precious metals and also speak to the shift in philosophy about time itself?'" Tom explains. "I was trying to communicate as simply as possible a fairly complex set of interchangeable and moving parts. The concept of the clock just popped."

There was also a dog involved. An eight-year-old black Labrador named Brubeck, to be specific.

"My secret ingredient is probably dog walks," Tom says.

"Brubeck doesn't talk," he adds. "When we go for a walk, he's quiet and getting the energy out. It's a good space for me to let my brain connect the different dots. When we were working on the ProfitTime project, there were a lot of four-mile walks, for sure."

There you have it. A peek behind the creative curtain and the canine inspiration that led to ProfitTime.

Thank you, Tom, and Brubeck.

CHAPTER 16

UNDERSTANDING THE "WHY" BEHIND PROFITTIME

I was super excited about the 2019 National Automobile Dealers Association (NADA) convention in San Francisco.

My anticipation owed to the official launch of Provision ProfitTime, our new investment value metric and methodology for managing used vehicles.

I had high hopes that dealers would see ProfitTime's Investment Score and The Trifecta for exactly what they were intended to be—a way for dealers, used vehicle managers, and appraisers/buyers to improve net profit and ROI by making decisions about each used vehicle based on its unique investment value.

I was not disappointed.

ProfitTime created significant buzz among dealers. We had

one of our strongest new product launches, as measured by the number of dealers who signed up at NADA.

In my view, ProfitTime was off to the races, and dealers and the used car business itself was moving to a better place.

But as I'm writing nearly eight months later, I've begun to realize that ProfitTime is putting some dealers back on their heels. They are not using the system to its fullest potential. They are not seeing the results—improvement in both net profitability and sales volumes—that are occurring for dealers who have successfully made the transition to ProfitTime.

I've thought long and hard about what distinguishes these two groups of dealers—those who try ProfitTime and fall short, and those who adopt ProfitTime and achieve results they did not expect.

The difference boils down to one thing—understanding the "why?" behind ProfitTime and using this understanding to fuel the operational changes that are necessary for ProfitTime to make a positive and significant difference.

The apparent lack of understanding about ProfitTime reminds me of the early days of vAuto and the Velocity Method of Management.

We saw a similar issue back then. Dealers would try Velocity, they'd find it difficult, and then they'd ditch it in favor of their old ways of doing business.

Eventually, nearly every one of those dealers came back to Velocity. They did so after recognizing the "why?" behind Velocity—that the Internet had created a far more efficient and transparent market that rendered traditional used vehicle pricing and purchasing practices obsolete.

Many dealers also realized that while they may have tried Velocity, they didn't *adopt* it. They used parts of the vAuto software to fit the way they were doing business. They did not use the software and Velocity principles to fundamentally change *how* they managed their used vehicle operations.

I'm seeing the same dynamic with ProfitTime today.

Dealers are taking pieces of ProfitTime, like the Investment Score or The Trifecta, and using them to make some decisions.

But they aren't using ProfitTime to fundamentally change how they think about the net profit and ROI potential of each vehicle, and subsequently manage their used vehicle operations accordingly. They are not using ProfitTime to solve for the loss of net profitability that often brought them to ProfitTime in the first place.

Over time, the dealers get frustrated. When they don't see the results, they often blame ProfitTime. They don't look in the mirror and ask what they could or should have done differently.

But the fact is, because these dealers never fully transitioned to ProfitTime, they were never in a position to enjoy the benefits it can deliver. They didn't invest the effort or time to undo the investment inversion in their inventory and apply ProfitTime's investment value insight to every decision they make on every used vehicle.

To me, these are all signs that the ProfitTime dealers who struggle aren't struggling with the tool, they're struggling with a lack of understanding of why they need to change the way they're doing business.

Think about it: If you're faced with a difficult task, which is most certainly true of the transition to ProfitTime, are you more or less likely to tackle the task if you don't know why you should?

We all should know the answer to the question—any one of us is less likely to do something, let alone something that's difficult, if we don't understand why it's important.

Based on the experiences of ProfitTime dealers so far, it's clear that transitioning to its investment value–based method of used vehicle management *is* hard.

That's the reason I'm writing this chapter.

It's my hope that if I distill the "why?" behind ProfitTime, it'll short-circuit the cycle of dealers signing up and failing to use ProfitTime to its fullest potential.

WHY #1: YOU CAN'T COUNT ON MAKING NET PROFIT IN USED VEHICLES ANY LONGER SIMPLY BY SELLING MORE CARS AND GENERATING MORE GROSS PROFIT

I don't know a single dealer who hasn't bemoaned the effects of margin compression in used vehicles.

As dealer Bill Knight aptly put it in chapter 7, the used vehicle business at his stores was starting to look like the new vehicle business—front-end gross profits and net profitability were steadily losing ground.

He, like other dealers, focused on a tried-and-true formula to fix the profitability—sell more volume to make up for the smaller front-end gross profits.

You might express the formula this way—V (volume) x G (gross) = NP (net profit).

But I would submit that this formula doesn't work anymore for three key reasons:

I. **USED VEHICLE NET PROFITS ARE TRENDING DOWN, NOT UP.** If the formula worked as well as many dealers believe it should, we'd be seeing different trendlines in the NADA financial data. We'd see that dealers are selling more cars, earning more total gross, and reporting a healthier net profit in their used vehicle departments.

> But that's not what NADA is telling us. In fact, it's quite the opposite. In the past few years, used vehicle net profits have been trending down. In 2018, NADA reported that the average dealership earned $6 in average retail net profit per used vehicle retailed.
>
> To me, the $6 signals that half of the dealerships in America lost money in their used vehicle departments last year, and the other half saw less net profit than the year before—even as dealers retailed record numbers of used vehicles.
>
> If any dealers reading this chapter don't believe me, I'd encourage you to look at your own financial statement and see what the net profit picture has looked like over the past few years in your used vehicle department.
>
> I suspect you'll find ample evidence that more than suggests the V x G = NP no longer works as well as it used to.

2. **VOLUME HAS ITS LIMITS.** The V x G = NP formula has another problem beyond the fact that it no longer generates the net profit dealers once enjoyed.

> The problem is that, in today's more competitive used vehicle market, there are natural limits to volume. There are only so many used vehicles that will retail in a year in a given market, and your competitors are increasingly less likely to allow you the sales volume that might generate sufficient gross profit to cover your net (after all, they're probably pursuing the V x G = NP formula, too).

3. **THE FORMULA FORCES YOU TO MANAGE THE WRONG THINGS.** It's curious to me that most dealers and used vehicle managers can't tell you the net profit their used vehicle department earned without looking it up. They'll know their volume. They'll know their gross profit. But they don't know their net profit unless they open their financial statement.

> It's a little odd that dealers, and used vehicle managers in particular, aren't aware of the single most important indicator of whether their used vehicle department is making a positive financial contribution to the dealership.
>
> But it's also understandable—we didn't need to know the net profit because, if we properly managed gross profit and volume, the net profit took care of itself.
>
> Today, however, gross profits are so low and

additional volume is so hard to get that dealers' efforts to manage these elements of the formula amount to pushing boulders up a steep hill.

You're working harder and harder to push the boulders to get to a better place, but, unfortunately, given today's market conditions, your effort is less and less effective.

Put another way, the gross deception is alive and well. Dealers are working harder than ever to sell more cars, yet they're losing money in their used vehicle departments.

The premise behind ProfitTime is that dealers should flip the formula. They should manage the net profit or ROI potential each used vehicle holds to ensure there's sufficient net profit left over after you sell a vehicle.

Dealers who struggle with ProfitTime often still have some vestige of the V x G = NP formula in play, and it's counterproductive to achieving the net profit and ROI improvements ProfitTime might otherwise deliver.

WHY #2: PROFITTIME PROVIDES A WAY TO MANAGE WHAT MATTERS MOST—YOUR ROI

If you had 10 dealers in a room and asked them if a $2,500 front-end gross was "good," everyone would say, "Yes."

But let's consider the $2,500 front-end gross in the context of two different deals.

With the first deal, you made the $2,500 gross on a $50,000 vehicle that sold after 60 days in inventory.

With the second deal, you made the $2,500 gross on a $20,000 vehicle that sold in 10 days.

If you asked the same 10 dealers to identify the deal that would make the most money for the used vehicle department and the dealership, they'd all likely point to the second deal, which is the correct answer.

But I would submit that if those deals occurred tomorrow at almost any dealership in the country, dealers and used vehicle managers wouldn't see the difference.

To them, each deal is "good" because it generated a satisfying $2,500 gross profit.

There's little, if any, recognition that the time it takes to earn the $2,500 makes a big difference in terms of the net profit or ROI each deal brings to the bottom line of the used vehicle department.

I view it as a significant problem that dealers and used vehicle managers do not have the capacity or understanding to discern the difference between the two deals.

The lack of ROI recognition is a big reason, I believe, that dealers are wondering why they're not making any money, or even losing money, in their used vehicle departments while selling record numbers of vehicles.

The ProfitTime methodology is entirely based on the idea that, in today's market, dealers simply must manage the net profit and ROI potential each used vehicle represents—a task that's impossible, by definition, if you don't recognize or account for the fact a vehicle's ROI is determined, in part, by the time it takes you to earn it.

As I tell dealers, many businesses do a lot of sales volume and yet lose money. In addition, there are many businesses that earn a lot of gross profit and lose a lot of money.

But if you show me a business that is making a positive ROI, you can bet the business is making money.

That's the whole point of ProfitTime, and it's one that gets lost when dealers and managers fall victim to a gross deception and fail to distinguish that the time it takes to make a $2,500 retail gross profit is a primary factor in determining whether it was truly good or bad for their business.

WHY #3: TODAY'S MARKET REQUIRES A SHIFT TO INVESTMENT MANAGEMENT

If I had a magic wand, I'd wave it over the heads of every dealer and used vehicle manager who has begun using ProfitTime.

By waving my magic wand, I'd instantly transform them from being astute inventory managers and turn them into astute investment managers.

Unfortunately, I don't have a magic wand, and the individuals who have become experts at inventory management seem to have trouble making the transition to becoming used vehicle investment managers.

Let's look at a couple of examples of why making this transition is proving difficult:

Example 1: You have a Bronze vehicle that just arrived in your inventory. If you're an inventory manager, it's a "fresh" car, full of profit potential. You'd take this understanding and probably arrive at an asking price that reflects your belief that the vehicle has plenty of retail shelf life.

By contrast, if you're an investment manager, you'd recognize that a Bronze vehicle has little or no net profit and ROI potential, and whatever amount it may have will dissipate quickly. You'd likely set an asking price that reflected your need to retail the vehicle as quickly as possible to maximize your ROI and reinvest in another vehicle.

Example 2: You have a Platinum vehicle that just arrived in inventory. If you're an inventory manager, you'd recognize that you're in the vehicle right, it's got the potential to retail quickly, and you price it to ensure a fast sale that might make up for the fact that you've got other distressed and older-age inventory that isn't moving.

By contrast, if you're an investment manager, you'd recognize that your Platinum vehicle is, for all intents and purposes, a "natural"—a vehicle with a low Market Days Supply, a low Cost to Market percentage, and high Retail Sales Volumes. It's a car that you know you more than likely don't have to sell on price because of its strong standing in the market. You set an asking price that reflects this innate market strength.

The differences between the decisions an inventory manager would make compared to an investment manager couldn't be more stark—and they point directly to a reason some dealers and used vehicle managers struggle with ProfitTime.

They have trouble managing the net profit and ROI potential

of each vehicle, and it often feels contradictory or foreign to the best practices inventory managers have applied for years.

When I explain the whys behind ProfitTime with dealers, I bring them back to a ProfitTime composite snapshot of their inventories.

We'll look at the percentages of Bronze and Silver vehicles that they've priced proudly and allowed to languish on the lot.

We'll revisit the Platinum and Gold vehicles and note how quickly they're moving out of dealer inventories—as if they're radioactive and need to be swept out right away.

Then I'll point to the composite column, which shows the average days in inventory for the Bronze and Platinum vehicles—let's say the average days in inventory is 25 for Platinum and 60 for Bronze vehicles.

I'll ask the dealer: If you flipped those numbers and your average age for Platinum vehicles is 60 and it's 25 for your Bronze vehicles, would you be making more money?

At this point in the conversation, the light bulb often goes on.

Dealers and used vehicle managers see the "why?" behind ProfitTime. They recognize that the way they've been managing their used vehicle inventories yields suboptimal results. They understand that while they may have had ProfitTime, the hands of traditional used vehicle inventory management held them back from applying ProfitTime's investment value insights to fundamentally change the net profit and ROI outcomes of individual vehicles.

This is also the point where I ask the dealers whether they're in or out with ProfitTime.

I'll stress that they don't need to change the way they're doing business. But I'll also emphasize that if they choose to stay the current course, they must recognize that the net profit pain they've been feeling will likely continue and even get worse.

Most dealers make the commitment. With the "why?" behind ProfitTime firmly in hand, they begin their journey to manage each used vehicle for the net profit and ROI potential each vehicle holds rather than the number of days they hold each unit.

Now let's examine what the ProfitTime journey looks like and the results it's bringing to dealers across the country.

CHAPTER 17

PROFITTIME IN PRACTICE—FIXING YOUR INVENTORY INVESTMENT INVERSION

B y its nature, the transition to ProfitTime is difficult for most, if not all, dealers.

The difficulty owes primarily to a fact of human nature—none of us like to face the music of financial losses.

But when dealers first turn on ProfitTime, that's exactly what's in front of them.

If they want ProfitTime to work, they've got to fix the inventory investment value inversion that's draining their used vehicle net profit and sales volume potential.

I've noticed, though, that the pain involved in fixing the investment value inversion seems less severe for some dealers compared to others.

The difference, I've learned, owes to how closely dealers manage their inventory levels based on their rolling 30-day total retail sales—the Balancing the Equation prescription we discussed in chapter 5.

If dealers are maintaining a 1:1 ratio between their inventory in stock and their rolling 30-day total retail sales, they most definitely will have Bronze vehicles in their inventories. But they will have fewer aged Bronze units to dispatch quickly as they fix the inventory investment inversion.

By contrast, if dealers maintain a 1.25:1, 1.5:1, or even a 2:1 ratio of inventory to their rolling retail total, they'll naturally have more vehicles that suffer the double curse of being both Bronze *and* over-age. By their nature, these vehicles are already suffering from deep financial distress, which makes reckoning with them right away more costly and painful.

This situation is exactly why, in a perfect world, I recommend that dealers work first to maintain as close to a 1:1 ratio of inventory to their rolling 30-day total retail sales before they turn ProfitTime on for the first time.

But we don't live in a perfect world, and the desire and motivation for dealers to adopt ProfitTime's net profit- and ROI-focused inventory management methodology is sometimes too strong.

Sometimes dealers feel they must tackle everything all at once.

I get it. I can be impatient too when I see a workable solution to a problem I know I need to fix—and fix sooner rather than later—right in front of me.

I'll caution dealers that balancing the inventory levels to your rolling 30-day total retail sales while transitioning to

ProfitTime makes doing both jobs doubly difficult. I'll warn that this course is a tall order for their teams and will test their change management skills.

But I'll also add that it can, and has, been done.

TAKING THE FINANCIAL MEDICINE

Steve Jackson, pre-owned director at Shaheen Chevrolet, Lansing, MI, would fall among the dealers who came to ProfitTime without an even balance between his inventory levels and his rolling 30-day total retail sales.

Jackson's department would consistently retail 200 vehicles with an inventory of 250 or so units.

When Jackson turned on ProfitTime in January of 2019, his inventory composite wasn't a pretty picture.

"Our average days to sale was 95 days, and 55 percent of our inventory was Bronze," Jackson says. "My Cost to Market on my Bronze and Silver vehicles was 103 percent. Sixty-five percent of our inventory was older than 60 days."

Jackson recalls the meeting with his dealer, the general sales manager, and others where he explained how he planned to fix the inventory investment value inversion. Jackson walked them through how he'd need to lower the prices on the Bronze and Silver vehicles from Price to Market percentages of 100 percent or higher, to Price to Market percentages of 95 percent and 96 percent or even lower.

The air went out of the room.

"Everyone went, 'Uh-oh,'" Jackson says.

"I repriced my Bronze and Silver vehicles and let the bleeding begin," Jackson says. "The department lost more than $100,000 in January and February. Those first two months were an utter bloodbath."

While Jackson was clearing out the distressed and aged inventory, he also worked to correctly price his Gold and Platinum vehicles—often raising the prices to Price to Market percentages that made him uncomfortable.

"My Performance Manager told me, 'You're not pricing your Platinum and Gold high enough,'" Jackson says. "I said, 'You're kidding me, right? You want me to price those at 103 percent and 104 percent Price to Market?' He said, 'Just do it. You'll see.' And he was right."

After the first two financially difficult months, Jackson began to see the investment inversion correct itself. The share of Bronze vehicles had diminished, in part because their more investment value–attuned prices translated to a faster pace of retail sales.

Meanwhile, he was more patient with Platinum vehicles, which meant he was making more money. "If you start them out with low prices, they sell too fast," he says.

Jackson also kept a close eye on inventory acquisition as he worked to align his inventory size more closely to his rolling 30-day total retail sales.

"I might need 20 Silverados," Jackson says. "But I know I don't really need them if they're all Bronze with scores of 1 or 2."

Four months later, the memory of the financial pain of Jackson's transition to ProfitTime remained sharp, but his financial statement is helping dull the edges of the pain.

"In July of 2018, we sold 216 used cars with about 250 units in stock, and our average front-end was $1,035," Jackson says. "The final net profit number hit and, after sales comp and everything, we made $6,000.

"Today, our average front-end is $1,550–$1,600 a copy, we're carrying 180 units and selling them," he adds. "We're going to sell 40 less cars and make $100,000 more than last year. It's like, 'Wow! That's good math.'"

On the other side of the inventory investment inversion scale, I'd put Jarred Black, general manager at Larry H. Miller Toyota Boulder (CO).

When he started to address his inventory's investment inversion in early 2019, he had long managed to retail about 100 used vehicles a month while carrying 100 or fewer vehicles in stock. The average age of his inventory was 23 days, and average Price to Market percentage across all vehicles was 98 percent.

"I've always operated on a pretty quick turn," Black says. "I've always had that mindset. I've sold 125 with 100 in stock, or 100 with 75 in stock. I never felt that to sell 150 that I needed 150."

Black's inventory velocity meant he had a smaller share of Bronze vehicles than other dealers (about 25 percent). Still, Black's inventory suffered from an investment inversion.

"We were inverted," he says. "Bronze cars were one way, and Platinum cars were another way. We went ahead and raised some of our pricing on Platinum vehicles and lowered our pricing on the Bronze vehicles."

Black estimates the Platinum vehicle price increases averaged $1,000, and the discounts on Bronze vehicles ran close to $2,000.

But while the adjustments brought some financial pain, they didn't send Black's bottom line tumbling into the red.

Instead, he and his team saw an almost immediate lift in sales volume and front-end gross profit.

"We had people coming in and buying the cars we'd raised the prices on," Black says. "We would have transacted at the lower price if we had left them the way they were."

In the months since the initial investment inversion fix, Black's department has seen sales volumes grow by 50 units a month (due largely to retailing through Bronze and Silver vehicles at a faster clip) and gross profits increase by $200 to $300/car.

"We learned really quick by going through that investment inversion exercise that ProfitTime is the real deal," Black says.

"In addition, ProfitTime is helping us in making a good decision on each car at the beginning," he says. "That's not to say we're not going to keep or acquire a Bronze car, but we need to make sure that from the beginning that we're on the money in terms of price. Those cars are still a big part of what we do."

STICKING TO THE PROFITTIME GAME PLAN

In addition to creating some up-front financial distress, the effort to fix your inventory investment inversion also brings personal and professional tests.

The tests arrive every time you see a vehicle's ProfitTime Investment Score and precious metal designation, and your inventory manager instincts kick in.

As I mentioned in the previous chapter, ProfitTime dealers often find that their instincts as inventory managers tell them to do things they shouldn't if they intend to stay true to ProfitTime's investment value–driven management methodology.

I thought it'd be useful to hear about these potential ProfitTime trouble spots—the times when inventory management and investment management diverge—directly from dealers.

"It's very hard to jump in to ProfitTime with both feet," says Lisa Groleau, sales manager at Bill Marsh Auto Group, Traverse City, MI. "What we found ourselves doing is being selective in using the ProfitTime model. We found excuses to go outside the model at first, which caused our grosses to dip. But once we went all in, it quickly raised the grosses back up."

I asked Groleau to clarify what she meant by being "selective" and going "outside the model."

Here's her take:

> "It's our own egos. It's hard to take that aged Bronze inventory right off the bat and slash our prices. Why? Because we know what we own it for. Every time you look at what you own it for, it makes it hard to price it right the first time.
>
> "You know, it's equally difficult for Velocity dealers. We've been trained over the years to not worry about the front-end gross part. We knew that we would just sell more cars faster and grow that total gross pot. But

> that makes it hard to mark up the Platinum cars. You have it in your head that you only need to make so much. So you price it that way and move on to the next car to free up that floorplan.
>
> "It's just as difficult to properly price the Bronze cars as it is for the Platinum vehicles.
>
> "It's about the entire model, and until you do it for 30 days, you're not going to see that success. But when you hit the 30-day mark, the success is almost instantaneous. It's like, 'This is incredible. I'm onto something.'"

I like how David Bishop, vice president of Bishop GMC Cadillac, in Cheboygan, MI, uses a football analogy to keep his decision making attuned to each vehicle's investment value and not the unit's days in inventory.

"ProfitTime is like the coach grabbing your face mask and saying, 'Hey! This is what you need to do,'" Bishop says.

For example, Bishop says that he's had to let go of a 15-day buffer he'd allow for vehicles, which ProfitTime might classify as Bronze or Silver, that might have been overserviced or required some reconditioning work that didn't get accounted for in the initial appraisal.

"I'd end up being a little less aggressive on the vehicles at first, and give them 15 days at a Price to Market of 100 percent before making gradual adjustments," Bishop says. "Now ProfitTime is saying, 'Hey, Dummy. You need to get this thing gone.'"

At his Toyota store in Boulder, Black says the most difficult part of his ProfitTime transition relates to Platinum vehicles.

"Our biggest issue was not being priced high enough on Platinum vehicles and not being patient," Black says. "Being patient means it's OK to price those vehicles higher and let them sit for 30 to 35 days because that's where you're going to make the extra money that will offset some of the Bronze and Silver vehicles."

Nearly every ProfitTime dealer or manager adds that ProfitTime's investment value–based management methodology also tests their sales teams. They are accustomed to seeing every fresh car start with an asking price that at least allowed them the opportunity to make some gross profit.

That's not necessarily the case with ProfitTime, especially with Bronze and Silver vehicles.

"Now, if a salesman is asking why we've only had this truck for five days and we're only going to make $500, I have a good answer," says Jackson at Shaheen. "It's because those trucks are Bronze or Silver. They need to sell quickly. It's get them in and get them out or we'll make even less."

It should be noted that some dealers aren't able to successfully fix their inventory investment inversion.

These dealers either shy away from facing the financial pain or taking the medicine, or they try to fix the inversion by applying traditional, Calendar Time–based inventory management practices, and they fail to adopt a more disciplined and strict adherence to the investment value insights ProfitTime delivers.

It's also true that dealers who successfully fix the inventory investment value inversion typically move into the next phase of their ProfitTime journey—sharpening, tightening, and tweaking their investment value–based priced strategies.

Let's have a look at how dealers set the parameters for proper ProfitTime pricing and take advantage of its opportunity.

CHAPTER 18

PARAMETERS OF PROPER
PROFITTIME PRICING

U sed vehicle manager Jim Mason at Steven Toyota, Harrisonburg, VA, quickly noticed that ProfitTime inspired him to pay more attention to how he priced his used vehicles than he had in the past.

It wasn't that Mason wasn't paying attention before. He was, and did.

Every day, Mason would click on his "Needs Attention" vehicles—the ones that Provision, his inventory management system, told him he should examine. The feature flags vehicles that require a closer look for reasons like a vehicle might be missing a price, or it hadn't seen a price change in seven days, or its competitive position might be off-target.

Mason would examine the "Needs Attention" vehicles, adding and adjusting prices when/where it made sense. Then he'd move on with the dozens of other items that he and his peers have on their daily to-do lists.

But ProfitTime has Mason doing things differently.

"Every day, I come in and I touch every car," he says. "I look at how it's doing and where it's sitting. I'm watching VDPs and SRPs [search result pages]. I make price adjustments if I need to. Eighty percent of the time, I'm moving prices down because of something I see in the competitive set; with the other 20 percent, I'm raising prices."

I asked Mason to draw out a couple of the key differences he's adopted with ProfitTime, compared to his Velocity pricing strategy.

"Before, I wasn't looking at my vehicles as much," Mason says. "I would look at my cars that were off-target and would do what I needed to do to get them on-target.

"But that was only some of the cars, and it can sometimes feel like brainless work," he adds. "With ProfitTime, I'm looking at every car, and it's added another layer to analyzing your inventory—how many Platinum cars do I have? When are they leaving? How am I doing on my Bronze cars? When are they leaving? I can now see these things, and it makes a difference."

Mason's experience is similar to what I'm hearing from other ProfitTime dealers and used vehicle managers. Their used vehicles are getting *more* attention.

This is a positive development on several levels. The additional attention dealers and used vehicle managers are paying to their used vehicles sets the stage for mastering what I've come to call the Parameters of Proper ProfitTime Pricing:

PARAMETER I: DAILY OVERSIGHT

First, I've always encouraged dealers to look at every vehicle, every day, to ensure its online position and price make sense.

Why? Because that's the way vehicle buyers look at your cars. If they're on the hunt, they're circling and clicking on cars that are part of their purchase set. And if they're interested in a car you carry, you'd want to do everything you can—which means eyeing every car, every day—to make sure your vehicle shows up on the consumer's hunting grounds.

Jarred Black, general manager at Larry H. Miller Toyota Boulder (CO), shares my perspective.

"The market changes every single day," Black says. "If you don't look at the car every day and see the market changed, and your customer looks at the car and sees that it became the second-best in terms of price, and they buy another car because you're too lazy to look at your cars every day and it cost you a car deal . . . that's not something I want at my store."

Black just made a point that's worth repeating and under-scoring—the market changes every day, and with ProfitTime, you see the movement more clearly.

The clarity comes because ProfitTime combines the volatility that is associated with Market Days Supply, Cost to Market, and Retail Sales Volumes. Dealers could look at each of these metrics individually and not necessarily see any notable change in a vehicle's competitive position online or its profit potential.

But since ProfitTime's algorithm blends all three metrics into one, you get a better picture of where each vehicle stands in your market and how much it may change over time.

"It's a little surprising to see how much the Investment Scores on cars are moving," Mason says. "This is after the ROs [repair orders] are closed, so my cost isn't changing. The market is changing for my cars. You have to keep an eye on them."

That's how Black thinks, too.

"ProfitTime has forced us to look at every car every day, and believe in what it's telling you," he says. "We understand the Investment Score and metal is going to change. It's doubtful it will change every day, but it changes. When we see that, we'll adjust the competitive set. If the vehicle's ProfitTime score or metal changes drastically, we'll adjust the pricing."

PARAMETER 2: PROPER COMPETITIVE SET POSITIONING

By now, almost every dealer understands that if a used vehicle isn't competitively priced, it isn't for sale.

This is true for every used vehicle—even Platinum cars. If you've got a competitive set of 15 other vehicles and you price a Platinum vehicle outside this range, chances are it may never find a buyer because you are, in effect, asking for the moon.

But the key question when it comes to pricing vehicles with ProfitTime is *how* competitively do you position vehicles in the context of their Investment Scores and precious metal designations?

To be sure, the right answer to this question depends on the dealer.

For example, if you're in a market where vehicle buyers want an easy and fast purchase process, the confidence to know they're getting at least a fair deal, and the sense that they'll get treated with utmost respect, the dealers who satisfy those wants and needs should have some latitude to believe that their vehicles don't have to be as competitively priced as the dealers' vehicles down the street.

Still, dealers with even the most spot-on and stellar reputations can't get away with asking for the moon. At some point, nearly every used vehicle buyer is budget- and price-conscious.

That's why, as dealers contemplate their competitive pricing sets in ProfitTime, they should always remember that vehicle buyers frame their own competitive sets, and it's your job to figure out where you need to be, in the context of those competitive sets, to earn the customers' interest and business.

I believe ProfitTime's Investment Score and precious metal designations help dealers figure out how competitively each car should be positioned in ways that are similar to and distinctly different from the pricing principles that are often associated with the Velocity Method of Management.

For example, if I were a Velocity dealer, the best practice would be to vRank every car 1, 2, or 3 every day. Your goal is to have every car fall among the top three best values for that vehicle to help drive a fast pace of Retail Sales Volume across your entire inventory.

But that's not the way I recommend dealers price with ProfitTime. Each vehicle's competitive position depends on its Investment Score or precious metal designation, as well as the specific context of the competitive set for each vehicle.

Let's take a Bronze car. If I were the dealer with a Bronze

car, I'd still want to rank it the way I would if I were a Velocity dealer—among the top three value rank positions in the competitive set. Why? Because it's a Bronze car and I need to get out of the vehicle really fast.

I've never thought that a vehicle should be priced below the competitive set—that wouldn't be my job as a dealer to essentially set the market floor. But I'd want to be certain that my car was priced and positioned to make the most of what is already a distressed inventory investment.

By contrast, if I'm a dealer with a Platinum car, I don't care what the calendar says. If it's Day 1 or Day 45, I'm not worried if it's a Platinum car. Why? Because I'm in the vehicle right enough, and the vehicle's a natural in the market based on its Market Days Supply and Retail Sales Volume. I don't need to be as competitive in the context of the vehicle's competitive set.

If the competitive set has 15 cars, I might not price it at 15, and I probably wouldn't price it above the #15 vehicle in the set. But I might price it at 12, 13, or 14, depending on the specific Platinum Investment Score.

I would also do the exact same things that Mason and Black are doing—looking at every car, every day, and watching how they move in the market.

Generally speaking, the Investment Scores of vehicles do go down over time.

If I have a Platinum car and it becomes a Gold car, I would reexamine the competitive set. I would probably see that I need to step down from the vehicle's position at 12, 13, or 14 in the competitive set.

Given it's a Gold car, I probably wouldn't want to push the vehicle's position down too far. I suspect I'd be comfortable at the 9th, 10th, or 11th position in the competitive set.

It's a similar dynamic if it's a Silver car. If I'm comfortable with putting a Gold car in the 9th, 10th, or 11th position in the competitive set, I'd probably rank the Silver vehicle at 5th, 6th, or 7th in the competitive set.

Get the picture?

With ProfitTime, every vehicle must be priced competitively every day, and each vehicle's competitive position must correlate to its ProfitTime Investment Score or precious metal in the context of the competitive set.

Most ProfitTime dealers will tell you that it isn't easy to make the transition from focusing on days on the calendar to basing your decisions on the Investment Score and precious metal designation ProfitTime puts on every vehicle it can.

This difficulty brings me to the third parameter of ProfitTime pricing.

PARAMETER 3: DON'T PANIC, AND DON'T PRETEND

After reading the prior chapter on how dealers fix their inventory investment inversion using ProfitTime, you've probably gained an appreciation that Bronze and Platinum vehicles pose the most difficulty for dealers to properly price based on their Investment Score.

That's because both types of vehicles trigger a two-step reaction for almost every dealer and used vehicle manager—they're prone to panic and then pretend.

Here's what I mean.

If it's a Bronze vehicle, it's tempting to do what dealers have been doing for years—panic about the vehicle's poor profit potential, and pretend it doesn't exist.

You can tell when a dealer or used vehicle manager has this problem—they often have an outsize share of Bronze vehicles that are priced far higher than they should be given the lower investment quality these vehicles represent.

If it's a Platinum vehicle, dealers tend to panic when a vehicle hits a specific age milestone in their inventory and move to lower the price. Next, they'll pretend the price reduction is warranted due to inventory age—which, as I've tried to establish throughout this book, has little relevance or bearing on a vehicle's investment value.

There's another panic and pretend trap that some dealers fall into while they're pricing their vehicles using ProfitTime.

The scenario goes something like this: For whatever reason, a vehicle's ProfitTime score and precious metal designation strike someone as not right. The individual may think the vehicle has more investment value than ProfitTime's prediction. Next, they'll adjust the competitive set to "right-size" the vehicle's ProfitTime score and precious metal designation.

To be sure, competitive set adjustments that prove counterproductive can be honest mistakes. You might mistakenly credit a car with equipment or features it doesn't possess, that make the vehicle look better in the eyes of the market and ProfitTime than the vehicle itself warrants.

But I don't see too many cases where the competitive set

adjustments made vehicles *worse* in terms of their ProfitTime scores and precious metal designations.

The fact that most, if not all, of the competitive set adjustments produce a better ProfitTime score and precious metal designation suggest there's at least some, shall we say, aspirational elements to the final pricing decision.

Overall, as I view the landscape of ProfitTime dealers and used vehicle managers who are committed to its investment value–based pricing methodology, I've been impressed.

Once they get past the initial bumps and stumbles, these dealers and used vehicle managers are fine-tuning their ProfitTime pricing strategies—and coming up with some rational and smart ways to maximize the ProfitTime pricing opportunity at their dealerships.

I've particularly liked how a handful of dealers have found ways to tie their ProfitTime pricing strategies directly to individual vehicle Investment Scores.

While these approaches may not work for every dealer, they do a good job of showcasing how dealers arrived at a ProfitTime pricing game plan that they consider optimal for their inventories and stores in their markets.

Let's have a look in the next chapter.

CHAPTER 19

ATTUNING YOUR PROFITTIME PRICING STRATEGY TO YOUR MARKET

Dealer Jim Blickle of Performance Toyota, Sinking Spring, PA, came to the car business after starting his professional career as an engineer.

Blickle was drawn to the avocation because it played to one of his strengths—he loved math and had a knack for working with formulas and numbers to solve problems.

When Blickle signed up for ProfitTime, he began to address the investment inversion ProfitTime had revealed in his inventory.

"We started adjusting from the top, the Platinum cars," Blickle says. "The first week, we raised the prices on 25 cars that were Platinum and Gold, and maybe a few Silvers. The first week we sold 15 of them for more money than we'd been asking.

"We were going like, 'Huh?!' These cars have been sitting

here for 30 and 40 days. We raise the prices and people come running. It's like I'm in the Twilight Zone."

But Blickle also knew that the front-end gross profit improvement he'd seen on the Platinum cars right away would get washed away once he started repricing the Bronze and Silver cars.

That's when Blickle dusted off his engineer's hat and began playing around with numbers to come up with a ProfitTime pricing formula.

"It was an all-day deal where I was playing around with cars in ProfitTime and looking for a formula. I was not trying to raise or lower the overall price of my inventory," Blickle says. "I wanted the overall Price to Market average to come out the same."

Blickle knew that the average Price to Market percentage for his inventory was 97.5 percent. From there, he examined the percentages of vehicles in each ProfitTime precious metal category and the rate of sales in each category.

Somewhere in Blickle's process of thinking about and tinkering with the numbers, a light bulb came on.

He realized with the right Price to Market baseline and the proper alignment of Price to Market percentages across the ProfitTime precious metal designations, he could use the Investment Score to calculate a vehicle's ProfitTime price point.

In talking with Blickle about the process he followed to devise his ProfitTime pricing formula, it's apparent that it's a product of the magic of a sharp mind working overtime on a problem. After enough time, he'd landed on a solution, even if he wasn't exactly sure of all the specific steps that brought him there.

Here's a look at Blickle's formula:

In ProfitTime, he starts every vehicle at a 92 percent Price to Market percentage. From there, Blickle simply adds the vehicle's Investment Score to determine the Price to Market percentage.

If it's a Bronze car, Blickle's Price to Market percentage will run between 93 percent and 95 percent.

If it's a Silver car, the Price to Market percentage will run between 96 percent and 98 percent.

If it's a Gold car, the Price to Market percentage will run between 99 percent and 101 percent.

If it's a Platinum car, the Price to Market percentage will run between 102 percent and 104 percent.

Blickle and his team are happy with the formula.

Used vehicle sales volume has grown by 25 percent, thanks to faster sales throughput of Bronze and Silver vehicles, and front-end gross profits have more than doubled to more than $1,600/vehicle, thanks to healthier returns on Platinum and Gold vehicles (and smaller, if any, losses due to distressed and over-age Bronze vehicles).

As Blickle steps back and evaluates his ProfitTime performance so far, he appreciates the gross profits he's now seeing on Platinum cars, and he's happy he's moving Bronze vehicles faster.

"It's important to recognize a Bronze is a Bronze and price it correctly from the beginning," Blickle says. "Before, we did what we always did: Let's raise the price for a couple of weeks and see if we get lucky. Well, we don't bother with that anymore."

But Blickle thinks the progress he's made with Gold and Silver cars, which make up almost 60 percent of his inventory, is having the most profound influence on his used vehicle department net profit.

"The bigger help is what we're doing with the Gold and the Silver cars," Blickle says. "We're just asking for more money than we were before. That's the biggest contributor."

I've focused on Blickle's pricing strategy for three reasons.

First, it's simple and easy to understand. That was Blickle's initial goal, and he nailed it.

Second, Blickle's approach fits perfectly with the broader strategic goal that should define every ProfitTime dealer's pricing strategy—your pricing should reflect each vehicle's Investment Score and precious metal designation and allow fine-tuning based on the unit's competitive set.

Third, Blickle gave me the OK to share it. It's a gesture that goes beyond goodwill. In ProfitTime, Blickle sees a broader opportunity for dealers to ensure they get the profit they deserve from every vehicle.

"If more dealers follow this approach, more dealers will stop giving away Platinum cars," he says.

SNAPSHOTS OF OTHER PROFITTIME PRICING STRATEGIES

As dealers adopt ProfitTime pricing strategies, it's important to remember that the strategy setting is an iterative process—that is, it's totally proper and right to expect that you'll test and tweak different approaches as you find the one that works best for your dealership and market.

There's also a natural progression to this process.

Most ProfitTime dealers focus first on their Platinum and Bronze vehicles, like Blickle did. This focus fits the first-priority status of correcting the investment inversion caused by improper pricing on both ends of ProfitTime's inventory investment scale.

After this stage, dealers begin to fine-tune how they're pricing their Gold and Silver vehicles. Over time with ProfitTime, these vehicles tend to grow into larger respective shares of your inventory.

In some cases, these vehicles are like the middle kids in large families. They may get overlooked and sometimes forgotten.

But their voices and perspective must be consistently heard and understood to every extent possible. If they aren't, your family's a little less optimal than it could or should be.

I've also noticed what might be called a "circle-back" stage with ProfitTime pricing. Once dealers and used vehicle managers have corrected their inventory investment inversion by repricing their Platinum and Bronze cars, and have fine-tuned their way to a sweet spot for Gold and Silver vehicles, they circle back to the Platinum and Bronze cars with an eye for more opportunity.

That's where Blickle finds himself nearly 10 months into his ProfitTime journey.

"We're not done yet," Blickle says. "There's still volume out there. I'm just getting into the Bronze business."

At Bishop GMC Cadillac, Cheboygan, MI, vice president David Bishop's ProfitTime pricing journey reflects the test-and-tweak nature of shifting from a days in inventory–focused strategy to one where a vehicle's net profit and ROI potential matter most.

When Bishop got started, he thought Platinum vehicles should be priced at a Price to Market percentage of 100 percent, Gold vehicles at 97 percent, Silver vehicles at 95 to 96 percent, and Bronze vehicles at 95 percent or less.

He's since made some adjustments to his Platinum and Gold categories—after realizing that some of his higher-scoring Silver vehicles actually retailed when their Price to Market percentages were in the high 90s.

With that insight, Bishop adjusted the upper parameter for Bronze vehicles to a Price to Market percentage of 96 percent, and bumped his Silver vehicles at Price to Market percentages between 97 percent and 99 percent. Meanwhile, the Price to Market percentage target for Gold vehicles is 100 percent, and for Platinum, 100 to 103 percent.

In addition to the improvements Bishop has seen in front-end gross and net profit for his used vehicle department, he also likes how the ProfitTime pricing strategy makes his job a little less stressful.

"With ProfitTime, we're not under the gun on very car," Bishop says. "ProfitTime tells us where we can be patient. It gives me peace of mind. We're not just rushing to get stuff gone all the time."

At Nissan North, Columbus, OH, used vehicle manager Dan Garwatoski took an approach similar to Blickle when he crafted his initial ProfitTime pricing strategy—he used what he knew about the Price to Market percentages where vehicles tended to retail as a guide for his ProfitTime strategy.

"As I went down through the buckets, I thought, well, if I have a Bronze car, where most of my cars are exiting at Price to Market percentages between 90 percent and 92 percent, then I've got to be priced in that range with Bronze cars," Garwatoski says. "If this is supposed to be a car that's got a low Market Days Supply and I own it right, and it's the right car for my market—it's Platinum or Gold—I should be able to transact in the upper 90s as a Price to Market percentage."

A FEW PROFITTIME PRICING PITFALLS

As dealers and used vehicle managers implement their ProfitTime pricing strategies, they will inevitably encounter some bumps or hiccups.

It's not uncommon for used vehicle managers to start feeling squirrely when Platinum vehicles reach a days in inventory threshold that makes them uncomfortable.

"Last week, we sold a 133-day-old Town and Country," Bishop says. "It had a Platinum rank. I knew to be patient. We made over $4,500 on the front-end. If it was a year ago, we probably would have sold it for $500 front-end profit."

It's also difficult, as I've mentioned in previous chapters, for dealers, sales managers, and others to treat Bronze vehicles for everything they are not—which is a unit that offers positive net profit and ROI potential.

"You've got to trust the metrics," affirms Steve Jackson, used vehicle manager at Shaheen Chevrolet, Lansing, MI. "For a lot of dealers and managers, they'll see a beautiful truck with leather, and they'll pay extra for it. Then they plug it in to ProfitTime, and it's a Bronze vehicle that scores three or less. It's hard to price that vehicle where it should be, but I've learned to let the metrics basically make the decision."

Such scenarios reflect that innate and natural tension that comes when you're stepping outside the comfort zone of Calendar Time–based used vehicle management, and letting vehicle investment values guide your decisions.

But perhaps the most difficult bump or hiccup dealers and used vehicle managers encounter when they transition to ProfitTime centers on the way they acquire their used vehicles.

That's because ProfitTime is a powerful and sometimes dangerous tool in the hands of untrained appraisers and buyers.

As we'll see in chapter 21, it can sometimes take months to get all the people who influence the cost of every used vehicle on board the ProfitTime train.

But before we dive into ProfitTime's change management challenge and opportunity, let's take a final look at one of the thorniest issues that arrives when dealers use ProfitTime to price used vehicles: How long can you let a Platinum vehicle sit?

CHAPTER 20

A QUICK POINT ON PLATINUM VEHICLE PUSHBACK

E ver since dealers began using ProfitTime, there hasn't been a week that's passed when I didn't have at least one conversation with dealers about their Platinum vehicles. The precursor to the conversation is fairly typical: I'll see that a dealer's Platinum vehicles aren't priced as proudly as they should be. Instead of pricing the vehicles at Price to Market percentages at 100 percent or higher, the dealer's Platinum inventory might be priced at Price to Market percentages in the high 90s.

Now, to be sure, this scenario might be perfectly rational. A dealer's market might be highly competitive, or the vehicle might be a near-new model that butts up against prevailing prices for new vehicles.

But then I'll look at the average days to sell for Platinum

vehicles and how it hasn't changed much from the day the dealers first started with ProfitTime.

In my mind, these conditions suggest a lack of comfort or patience with pricing Platinum vehicles where they should be.

On one hand, the lack of comfort or patience is completely understandable. For many years, ProfitTime dealers followed a turn-and-earn strategy for managing their used vehicle inventories. It was rare, if not unheard of, to price vehicles above 100 percent on purpose (and not because you were trying to make up for overpaying or overreconditioning a vehicle).

But on the other hand, I don't hear rational reasons when I ask dealers questions about why they're pricing Platinum vehicles so aggressively and selling them so quickly.

The most common response is, "If I price the Platinum vehicles at a Price to Market percentage of 100 percent or higher, I won't get any Vehicle Details Page (VDP) views. If I don't get VDPs, how can I sell the car?"

That's when I'll remind dealers of two facts about properly pricing Platinum cars.

The first fact is that Platinum cars are, by definition, "naturals" in your market. They don't necessarily need the same number of VDPs as other vehicles. In fact, Platinum vehicles will transact with far fewer, if any, VDP views at all, because consumers are actively looking for these vehicles.

The second fact is that Platinum vehicles represent a dealer's best opportunity to maximize front-end gross profit, and if they aren't given sufficient time to earn the front-end gross, they'll never realize it.

The pushback on this point often comes in the form of a, "Yeah, but . . ." That is, dealers and used vehicle managers will say, "Yeah, but if I don't sell the Platinum cars quickly, I won't get the volume I need for the month."

It's at this point that I direct the dealer's or used vehicle manager's attention to their Bronze and Silver vehicles, where I often will find longer-than-acceptable metrics for days in inventory, and pricing that's too rich for the investment value these vehicles represent.

I'll then ask the dealers if they were more aggressive with the pricing and desire to retail their Bronze and Silver vehicles, would they feel less pressure to sell off the Platinum vehicles and effectively leave money on the table?

In most instances, the dealers get my point and begin to treat Platinum vehicles with a sharper understanding that these units are their most valuable used vehicle investments.

I also run into a lot of questions about whether it's OK for a Platinum vehicle to reach 70, 90, or even 100 days in inventory or longer.

I'll use this question to remind dealers that if a vehicle is truly a Platinum vehicle, its strength in the market, in terms of Market Days Supply and Retail Sales Volume, would suggest it shouldn't take that long to sell.

By definition, every Platinum vehicle represents an investment that you own really right, a salesperson can make a big commission on the car by selling it, it's got high demand and low supply, and it's got high Retail Sales Volume in the market.

Why would a vehicle like that be around so long?

Now, it's entirely possible that some Platinum vehicles may take three months or more to sell.

But I would consider these outliers. They aren't your bread-and-butter Platinum cars.

For most Platinum vehicles, if they haven't sold in 60 days, I'd submit the vehicle suffers from one of two problems.

The first problem is that the vehicle may well be overpriced—a scenario that could be due to a lack of daily attention to the vehicle's position in the competitive set (a ProfitTime pricing parameter we discussed in chapter 18).

Remember, competitive sets change all the time, and it's possible that the competitive set for a Platinum vehicle changed and, without you knowing it, your Platinum vehicle is no longer price competitive.

The second problem is that something may well be wrong with the vehicle itself.

I encourage dealers to go out and smell the car, run the car, and take a closer look at the car. The goal would be to figure out why salespeople seem to be walking around a car that they should rightfully want to sell.

Perhaps the best takeaway I can offer for properly pricing Platinum vehicles is to be patient with your pricing plan and position, but verify that it's always right for each vehicle.

OK, enough of the soapbox.

Now let's turn our attention to the ways ProfitTime helps dealers and used vehicle managers make better, more investment-minded acquisition decisions.

CHAPTER 21

USING PROFITTIME TO MAKE MORE INVESTMENT-MINDED ACQUISITIONS

I mentioned in chapter 19 that ProfitTime is both a powerful and dangerous tool when acquiring used vehicles.

I'll use this chapter to unpack both sides of that statement.

HOW CLARITY DRIVES PROFITTIME'S POWER

ProfitTime's power comes from the clarity it brings to used vehicle acquisitions.

For the first time in what I believe is the history of the used vehicle business, dealers and used vehicle managers can now appraise a vehicle and know, with crystal clear certainty, the quality of the investment that's before them in the context of its market appeal and their inventory mix.

The certainty and clarity comes from ProfitTime's Trifecta,

166   GROSS DECEPTION

the Investment Score, coupled with the Letter Grade and Strategy Action—the primary topic in chapter 14, which may be worth rereading in case you need a refresher.

I'm told The Trifecta is intuitive. Appraisers and buyers understand ProfitTime's 1–12 Investment Score point scale. They also know that they *should* know how well a market likes a vehicle and whether a dealer needs the unit in inventory and, if so, how badly, before they buy a car.

Perhaps the best part of The Trifecta is that it puts all the critical insights about each vehicle in front of every appraiser or buyer in one place.

If appraisers and buyers choose to take or purchase a vehicle, they know why they did it and what they've got. If they walk away, they know the reasons to justify the decision.

The clarity and understanding about each vehicle's ProfitTime Investment Score and its precious metal designation also sets the stage for a greater understanding, among all parties, of what a vehicle will mean as a retail piece once it's in your inventory.

"One of the coolest benefits of having ProfitTime in the showrooms is it really disintegrates excuses," says Trent Waybright, vice president of pre-owned operations at Kelley Automotive Group, Fort Wayne, IN. "It clears up the gray area. It really shows the guys and the buyers, when we're appraising the unit, for whoever or whatever it might be, and having the visible score and the metal right there in front of them, what's going to happen with that car when we get it in.

"There's so much data on the vAuto appraisal screen,"

Waybright adds. "I think a lot of the managers would look at it and move on; it's not a big deal or it's too much information. Now, they see a vehicle is a 2 or whatever it is. There are absolutely no surprises when it comes into their inventory, and I price it according to the score and metal the next morning."

The shared understanding also brings another benefit—a more concerted effort to appraise vehicles for the right money, based on the Investment Score and Trifecta insights, and acquire them right.

"At our Buick store, they're trying to engineer the appraisal process in the showroom with the buyers before we buy the car," Waybright says. "We never really had that before."

For example, the used vehicle manager at Waybright's Buick store now takes part in what they call "active appraisals." That is, when time allows, the manager walks a car with the customer and rides in it with them. The interaction is friendly and honest, and it usually gives customers an understanding of how and why the manager arrived at an appraisal number.

Waybright credits the approach for helping the Buick store maintain a more profit-productive Cost to Market percentage on trade-in units, 85 percent, that's 3 percent better than the group's Chevrolet store. The difference translates to a positive, nearly $400/vehicle difference in front-end gross profit on trade-in units at the Buick store.

Put another way, the store's active appraisal process is helping the dealership take in more Silver, Gold, and Platinum vehicles.

"I'm of the opinion that the trade-ins are going to be at least Silver, along with a lot of Gold and some Platinum," Waybright says. "Whereas the purchase units we get from auctions are pretty much all Bronze."

The observation proves accurate when you look at Waybright's acquisition data.

"Our entire world has changed with acquisition," he says. "With our centralized buying, we always felt we had an advantage, a major advantage, in our acquisition Cost to Market, being able to find the cars at auction at the right cost. That's greatly shifted. Our Cost to Market for purchased units at our Buick store was 82 percent in 2015. This year it's up to 87 percent, where it's been hovering."

Waybright's data echoes the discussion about the rise of the New Math in chapter 4, and it points to another reason ProfitTime is a critical tool for acquiring vehicles—it's increasingly difficult to get vehicles with a satisfactory net profit and ROI potential from the auction.

Hence, you need to make doubly sure you're doing everything you can to get your share of Silver, Gold, and Platinum vehicles when customers bring them to your door.

That realization is gaining ground among ProfitTime dealers.

At Shaheen Chevrolet in Lansing, MI, pre-owned director Steve Jackson says ProfitTime is providing the catalyst to "never miss a trade" and overpay for trade-ins less often.

A year ago, the Look to Book ratios for his appraisers ran around 45 percent. In mid-2019, it's 60 percent.

"The managers have learned to put the correct information in on the car in an appraisal," Jackson says. "Speed is half the issue. I get a notification on my phone with every appraisal. If there's one in question and we need to be careful, I give them a call.

"If it's a Bronze or Silver car, I communicate right away to make sure we have the right money. They can see the ProfitTime score and metal, and if I'm calling, it doesn't necessarily mean that they put too much money in it. My biggest thing is to make sure we don't ever, ever, ever miss a car. There are not many appraisals that come in that aren't at least a high Silver.

"If they call me or a manager for a bump, I'll bump a Gold or Platinum car all day long just to get it," says Jackson, noting that the bumps typically amount to $400 or $500—enough money to make the deal and not significantly alter the ProfitTime metrics.

Jackson adds that they've tweaked their trade-in appraisal process to ensure that a used vehicle manager always gets involved when a trade-in requires a bump, and that a manager presents the first pencil, which is typically based on Kelley Blue Book Instant Cash Offer figures.

"We haven't been getting burned by appraisals unless somebody does a dumb thing," he says. "The ProfitTime metrics work if you put all the information in correctly. Before, it was essentially just rob the used car department and put whatever it takes into the car to get a deal done."

Such positive ProfitTime experiences illustrate how an investment value–based mindset can produce profit-favorable results when it comes to acquiring cars.

I would add that ProfitTime doesn't necessarily solve the problem Waybright highlighted—that it's extremely difficult to find and purchase auction vehicles, particularly when they come from captive financial companies that seem to want the moon for their inventory.

Still, ProfitTime assures that, even if you're looking at a Bronze vehicle at auction, you know exactly what you've got and how to handle it from a pricing and retailing perspective, if you choose to acquire it.

A DANGEROUS SIDE TO PROFITTIME

But there's another side to ProfitTime that I describe as dangerous.

We built the ProfitTime tool to ensure that dealers and used vehicle managers are as well informed as they can be about every vehicle's net profit and ROI potential.

We understood that the tool would help dealers make better acquisition decisions by bringing the clarity of each auction or trade-in vehicle's investment value front and center in the appraisal and purchase process.

Indeed, ProfitTime dealers *have* seen the investment values of their inventories improve. It's not uncommon, after ProfitTime dealers hit their stride, that their inventories benefit from a larger share of Platinum, Gold, and Silver vehicles, and a smaller share of Bronze units.

The specific distribution of these precious metal designations truly depends on the dealer. In some markets, you may always have a third of your inventory as Bronze vehicles. It's not that these vehicles are distressed due to age.

The problem, more often than not, is that the Bronze designation resulted from what a dealer paid to acquire the vehicle.

As Waybright noted, it seems like it's impossible to find and purchase anything other than a Bronze vehicle at auction—particularly if your customers want the late-model stuff everyone else does.

And therein lies the danger of ProfitTime.

The tool and Trifecta can be used to engineer unproductive outcomes.

For example, some dealers will make a conscious decision *not* to acquire any Bronze vehicles, whether at auction or trade-in.

It's not for me to judge whether the decision is right or wrong.

But it strikes me as another form of gross deception that's risky, particularly if you're in a market where, as I've seen with many dealers, Bronze vehicles are volume cars—the ones that help you meet your monthly sales volume targets and make at least some money if you retail them quickly. The faster throughput of Bronze vehicles also supports your right to give Gold and Platinum vehicles sufficient time to earn the premium net profit and ROI potential they deserve.

There's also some risk in putting a first pencil in front of customers with a Gold- or Platinum-level appraisal figure *every single time.*

If you do, you risk losing the increasingly precious opportunity that every trade-in vehicle represents. If customers think you're trying to undervalue their trade-in, you may not have a chance to offer the Bronze- or Silver-level appraisal their vehicle may well warrant.

Jarred Black, general manager for Larry H. Miller Toyota (Boulder, CO) would agree:

"Some people, when we look at the ProfitTime score and

precious metal, go, 'Are we not supposed to buy a Bronze car, or do we make the value lower to make it a Silver or Gold car?'" Black says. "My response is, 'Absolutely not. We just need to make sure that we are not changing our philosophy on the other side of it when we price and sell the vehicles.'"

I would submit, as a corollary to this thought of avoiding Bronze vehicles, that if your current Look to Book ratios on trade-ins are not at or above 50 percent, you probably haven't earned the right to set a "no Bronze car" rule and risk losing the opportunity to own and retail those vehicles.

Ultimately, my guidance to dealers who use ProfitTime's Investment Score and Trifecta to acquire vehicles is to remember that, at some level, every used vehicle simply is what it is, and you should accept it as such.

In life, it's dangerous to look at a spouse or significant other and say: "I don't like this or that about you, but I know I can change it to suit me better."

I believe the same thing is true in the used vehicle business, where the market tends to mold dealers, and dealers get in trouble when they try to mold the market.

As I close this chapter, I want to underscore that every successful implementation of ProfitTime into the used vehicle acquisition process requires dealers and used vehicle managers to bring their teams around to the idea of doing things differently.

It isn't easy, and it takes time.

But thankfully, ProfitTime dealers have some pointers to share in the next chapter.

CHAPTER 22

PROFITTIME'S CHANGE MANAGEMENT OPPORTUNITY

I've noticed a striking difference in the way dealers are adopting ProfitTime compared to the early days of Velocity adoption.

The difference is I'm not seeing as many heads roll as a result of the transition.

At one time, years ago, it seemed like almost every dealer got rid of a used vehicle manager who was too tied to tradition and couldn't (or refused to) see the value of the Velocity Method of Management.

But so far I'm not seeing the same dynamic today, which is a positive thing that owes to at least three factors:

I. DEALERS UNDERSTAND THAT BUY-IN IS BETTER WHEN THEY GIVE IT PATIENCE AND TIME. If you think about the past decade or so in the car business, every dealership has been awash in a sea of change. Whether it's changing to a different dealership management system (DMS), installing a customer relationship management (CRM) system, or bringing more digital elements into your new/used vehicle sales processes, the technology-driven nature of today's car business has forced dealers to become leaders and managers of change, whether they like it or not.

> I can think of several dealers who, over the years, managed to shed their "my way or the highway" style of leadership to one that's more accommodating to experimentation and, yes, even failure.
>
> I know this shift in management style can be difficult, particularly for dealers who, like me, tend to get impatient when we aren't seeing the progress toward a goal that we'd like as fast as we'd like.
>
> But, as dealer Ryan Sodikoff of Steven Toyota, Harrisonburg, VA, puts it: "There are different folks doing different strokes, even in my organization. It's our job to figure out how to get everybody on the same page, and know that you can't snap your fingers and have it happen all at once."

2. **THE COST OF TEAM CHANGEOVER IS BETTER UNDERSTOOD.** I have absolutely no statistical evidence to back up this assertion, but I'll share it anyway: While turnover remains chronically high at many dealerships, I would estimate that the

vast majority of the dealership team departures owe to someone giving up rather than a dealer or general manager firing someone out of anger or impulse. I may be wrong, but I just don't see as many tirades about used vehicle performance that I did in the past.

> I'd like to believe that this is because dealers, while they could, as a whole, create more people-positive work cultures and environments, do understand that bringing people along, rather than blowing them out at the first sign of struggle, is a better long-term strategy. It ensures they don't gain a reputation as an erratic place to work, and paves the way to hire and retain the right kind of people for the long haul—a far more profit-friendly solution than choosing to fight the ongoing costs of human capital inefficiency.

3. **DEALERS ARE STARTING IN A BETTER PLACE.** When Velocity first came on the scene, dealers had to fight two battles as they moved their teams to adopt it. First, there's the understanding of a new philosophy and how it plays out in used vehicle management decisions. Second, there's learning a new tool and all the market data associated with it for the very first time.

> While ProfitTime most definitely requires that dealers, used vehicle managers, and their teams come to understand a new investment value–based method of

inventory management, they are long accustomed to using the underlying tools.

In this way, they are starting their ProfitTime adoption in a better place. While the investment value-based methodology may challenge their inventory manager instincts, they already know their way around the solution that provides the new investment value insights they need to do the job right.

Of course, I also see some keen similarities between ProfitTime and Velocity adoption—beyond the fact that it's difficult and disruptive to the status quo.

Just like Velocity adoption, the transition to ProfitTime requires buy-in from all quarters. New cars. F&I. Service. Parts. Everyone must be on board and understand why you're doing things differently and how they'll benefit from the change, in the most personal terms possible.

In my discussions with dealers who have found success with ProfitTime, I've asked them to share some pearls of wisdom that might help other dealers better manage the transformative change that ProfitTime requires.

Here are a few for consideration:

Constant, constructive communication is critical. I'd recommend that every dealer who comes to ProfitTime establish at least once-a-week meetings with new/used vehicle department appraisers and managers, the service manager, and the F&I manager to review appraisals and discuss ways to make ProfitTime work better.

It's through these open, constructive conversations that everyone learns how to do their jobs better in the context of ProfitTime's goals and objectives.

Some may wonder why the F&I and service managers need to be part of the discussion.

In my view, it's important for both to know which vehicles ought to be higher priorities, based on their investment value, for their respective departments.

Take advantage of your teachable moments. ProfitTime is a journey where every forward step brings you closer to the destination.

When dealers roll out ProfitTime, it's not uncommon to have the experiences I've shared in prior chapters—that you raise prices on Platinum cars, and you suddenly have buyers purchasing the vehicles and sales associates making good commissions.

These are teachable moments.

If the Platinum car came from an auction, the buyer should know that he/she did a good job setting up the used vehicle department to make some money. Likewise, if it's a trade-in, the appraiser should know that they did right by the used car department.

In either case, the sales managers and teams should also know how ProfitTime, in the hands of buyers and appraisers, made their paycheck possible.

Here's another teachable moment.

Let's say a buyer or manager just acquired a Bronze vehicle with a score of 1, and your ProfitTime pricing strategy requires that you advertise an asking price that represents a retail loss. They need to know about it. Similarly, your sales team needs to know and understand why the car won't give them any gross opportunity.

As a change management leader, it's your job to help them understand how they arrived at the decision and how it could be different and better for the used vehicle department's bottom line the next time.

Emphasize the upside and the endgame. If there's one chapter in this book that might be mined for change management purposes, it would be chapter 16, where I lay out the case for why ProfitTime matters for dealers.

In my view, dealers who adopt ProfitTime are doing nothing short of preparing their dealership for future success in a market where margin compression and transparency are countervailing winds.

Everyone on your team should understand ProfitTime's importance to your business. In some ways, it ensures they'll all have jobs in the months and years ahead.

But it's also important for everyone to understand that ProfitTime isn't just about helping dealers make more money and providing job security—it's about advancing the opportunity for everyone in the dealership to earn more and share in a success that grows stronger with the committed participation of every player on your team.

In closing, I'll reemphasize that the change management associated with ProfitTime adoption is no small task. It's not likely to result in an overnight success. It may well feel, at times, like a slog with no end in sight.

But I can say with utmost confidence that dealers and used vehicle managers who successfully lead the change to ProfitTime reap its rewards.

As I talk to ProfitTime dealers who have turned the corner, most share that, in addition to helping them make more money and sell more used vehicles, ProfitTime has brought the fun back into the business.

I think the dealers would also agree that with ProfitTime, there's no "me" in the used car success it delivers, but there's an "us."

EPILOGUE

A BROADER VIEW OF PROFITTIME IN PROGRESS—AND A PROMISE

I'm grateful that you chose to read *Gross Deception*, and I hope it'll help you and your team find greater profitability and success with ProfitTime.

After I finished the book's manuscript, I realized there are a few emerging and potentially important observations that should be offered about ProfitTime and its progress in the market.

I'll share these observations with a caveat—what you read below may not be how things ultimately play out.

But, at least for now, the observations below should help dealers spot and address what may be opportunity or even trouble on the horizon.

Diversification of used vehicle acquisitions. In gathering the experiences and stories that make up this book, I couldn't help but be struck by how many dealers in different parts of the country are finding that acquiring auction vehicles has almost become a money-losing proposition—or at least one where the margins dealers once made are mere shadows of their former selves.

Dealers are smart. They're diversifying the way they acquire cars. Some are becoming Buying Centers for Kelley Blue Book or other companies. Some are using buyer groups/networks that specialize in acquiring inventory for dealers.

Time and again, I hear stories about how hard used vehicle buyers and managers are working to find vehicles that, when you plug them into ProfitTime, are probably not the kind of cars the dealer principal would prefer that you purchase.

Perhaps the situation represents a need for a shift—from working harder to addressing *how* you are working and where you're hunting for inventory.

A broader market price correction. I've noticed a positive trend as I evaluate the inventories of ProfitTime dealers during and after their transition to its investment value–based management methodology. Over time, the overall Price to Market percentage of their inventory rises.

This dynamic occurs in stages. Once dealers start on ProfitTime, the cumulative effect of correcting their inventory investment inversion tends to lower the overall Price to Market percentage, since there are typically more Bronze cars bringing the metric down than Platinum cars that might cause it to increase.

But once the investment inversion gets corrected and dealers retail their Bronze vehicles faster, the overall Price to Market percentage seems to increase and sustain itself due to larger shares of better-grade vehicle investments.

To be sure, the rise is more pronounced at some dealerships than others—perhaps a sign that some dealers were too aggressive with their previous pricing strategies.

But I wonder if there may be something bigger at work—the beginnings of a market price correction in used vehicles that results when you whittle away the gross deception that made dealers' overall Price to Market percentages lower than they needed to be.

In any case, the upward movement is a positive for dealership margins. Time will tell if it stays that way, but I'm encouraged by the current direction.

Investment-minded reconditioning. In chapter 22, I noted how service managers should be part of ProfitTime transition meetings. It's important that they understand that, from an investment perspective, some vehicles are worth more than others—and that they may need to re-jigger their reconditioning processes to ensure that the most net profit- and ROI-distressed Bronze and Silver vehicles need to be a top reconditioning priority.

This shift in priorities comes easiest to service departments that have already done the heavy lifting of changing their processes to get cars through the shop and retail ready in a matter of hours, not days or weeks.

I also believe that ProfitTime's investment value insights will spur dealers, used vehicle managers, and service directors to reconsider the cost of what must be done to every vehicle, given its investment value.

Pay plan pressures. As dealers see success with ProfitTime, some are finding that they need to adjust their pay plans to reflect the fact that front-end gross profits are no longer as anemic as they have been in recent years.

For Velocity dealers in particular, it wasn't uncommon for some to shift away entirely from commission- and gross profit–based pay plans to ones that emphasized sales volume targets.

But as ProfitTime helps dealers grow the gross profits and sales volumes, dealers are finding that they need to adjust pay plans to strike a better balance between their gross profit, volume, and base salary components.

This work means that some dealers are trimming back the bonuses they awarded when sales associates hit specific volume targets, and increasing the share of compensation that comes from gross profit or salary.

Today, some former Velocity dealers are moving back to pay plans that rely on gross profit to account for a larger share of sales associate and sales manager paychecks.

I would encourage dealers who transition to ProfitTime to keep a close eye on their pay plans. You may well find they become a pressure point for your department's net profit that needs to be adjusted.

The problematic nature of packs. Talk about another gross deception. I've long argued that dealers who pack their used vehicles beyond $200 to $400 are effectively pretending that the gross profit inherent in a vehicle doesn't really exist.

I've stressed that this practice makes appraisers and buyers gun shy or, even worse, makes them not give two hoots about the cost of a vehicle and its effect on the used vehicle department's bottom line.

The same could be said for sales associates who begrudge the fact that the dealer's pack crimps their ability to make a decent commission.

The whole point of ProfitTime is to give dealers a clearer view of each vehicle's net profit and ROI potential—a view that packs, by their nature, obscure.

Third-party influence on vehicle price/value perceptions. There's new concern and conversation about third-party classified sites as dealers begin using Provision ProfitTime.

The dialogue relates to the practice among third-party sites to rank or designate a used vehicle's asking price as great, good, fair, or overpriced.

ProfitTime dealers are wondering, if not worrying, about how these practices affect consumer perceptions of their used vehicle pricing, particularly as it relates to Platinum and Gold vehicles.

A quick refresher: As I've highlighted in earlier chapters, once dealers start with ProfitTime, their first order of business is to correct their inventory investment inversion. Using the net profit and ROI insight for each vehicle that ProfitTime provides, dealers will raise the asking prices for Platinum and Gold vehicles and lower the asking prices for Bronze and Silver vehicles.

Now, ProfitTime dealers worry that, as they raise the asking prices of their Platinum and Gold vehicles, the third-party sites will tell consumers the prices aren't fair, and the dealer will lose out on a potential deal.

To be sure, ProfitTime dealers aren't the first to raise the yellow flag on third-party classified site price ranks and designations and their potential impact on customers. If you scout dealer discussion sites online, the subject's been around for some time.

But I'm disturbed and troubled by how the discussion is quickly becoming prevalent among ProfitTime dealers in the closing weeks of 2019. The frequency makes me wonder if dealers are onto something.

Is there a disconnect between the competitive sets and market data dealers use to price their used vehicles, and the competitive sets third-party classified sites use to rank or value the dealer's asking price for potential buyers?

Unfortunately, as this book is going to press, I don't have a good answer.

I would like to believe, however, that the algorithms and formulas the third-party sites use to rank or value a used vehicle's asking price are based on relevant and valid market data. Further, I would also like to believe that the third-party sites actively seek to balance the interests of the dealers who advertise vehicles on their platforms and the consumers who use the platforms to find their next vehicle.

But one thing *is* certain.

I haven't heard that ProfitTime dealers are having trouble selling their Platinum and Gold vehicles at higher asking prices than these vehicles might have received in the past. In fact, the more common refrain is that dealers are surprised by how much interest their Platinum and Gold vehicles generate in a market even with higher asking prices.

I believe this reality owes to a couple of factors, which I share with dealers to put their minds at ease about any undue negative influence that may be caused by the rankings and designations third-party classified sites assign to used vehicle prices.

First, I'm not fully convinced that a third party classified site's price rank or value designation makes or breaks a deal with most used vehicle buyers and shoppers.

To be sure, some buyers and shoppers may see a third-party site's price rank or value designation and decide, "That's it. I'm going to buy this car."

But most consumers, I believe, will take a third-party site's price rank or value designation as but one reference point on their used vehicle purchase journey.

They will continue to look at other vehicles, and crisscross the third-party sites and their price rankings and designations, as they affirm for themselves what the right vehicle and right price may be.

I'll also tell dealers that if they're worried about the third-party classified site price ranks and designations for their Platinum and Gold vehicles, they should recognize that such indicators can help them as they price their Bronze and Silver vehicles more aggressively to match their respective investment values.

Second, I'll remind dealers that their Platinum and Gold vehicles don't need to be sold on price as much as other vehicles. As I've shared earlier in the book, Platinum and Gold vehicles are "naturals."

They are vehicles that sales associates have an incentive to sell, because you own the vehicles right and they offer a sizable commissionable gross profit; they have high demand and low supply in the market; and they have strong Retail Sales Volumes.

In other words, your Platinum and Gold vehicles are scarce and sought-after, and their buyers know it. It's my belief that these buyers are less likely to be influenced by a third-party site's price rank or value designation, especially if they've found the car they really want.

It's curious to me that the concerns and questions about third-party classified site price rankings and designations seem to be gaining steam at the same time ProfitTime is helping a growing number of dealers price their used vehicles to optimize each unit's net profit and ROI potential.

It may be just a coincidence, or it may be a sign of a larger problem.

That's why I'm encouraging dealers to pay closer attention to how third-party classified sites partners regard their ProfitTime pricing strategies. You should know how these sites regard your pricing decisions, and whether the rankings and designations make sense for what you also should know about your used vehicles, your market, and your customers.

Then, if something doesn't seem fair or right, it's time to start asking questions.

MY PROFITTIME PROMISE

As I mentioned in the book's introduction, I've made ProfitTime and its success among dealers a personal mission. That's a primary reason I undertook the task of writing this book.

But my mission is also a promise to you: As ProfitTime progresses in the marketplace, I'll be keeping close tabs and sharing what I learn and see.

As we all move forward, I'd encourage you to visit www.dalepollak.com for updates, or reach out to me directly at dpollak@vauto.com.

Thank you again for reading this book.

I hope and trust the book helps you get past the gross deceptions of today's car business, understand the new truths of used car profitability, and perhaps set the stage for your own tale of ProfitTime success.

ABOUT THE AUTHOR

DALE POLLAK was born into the car business.

His father, Len Pollak, started as an independent used vehicle dealer before owning a Buick-American Motors-Jeep-Renault dealership in Gary, Indiana.

After graduating from the Kelley School of Business at Indiana University in Bloomington, Dale joined the family business. He and his father opened Pollak Cadillac in Elmhurst, Illinois, in the early 1980s.

At the Cadillac store, Dale managed the used vehicle department, a job that led to two entrepreneurial opportunities.

The first came in the mid-1990s, as the internet spawned websites like AutoTrader.com and Cars.com. Dale understood the importance of getting his used vehicles listed online, and spent countless hours manually entering data on individual vehicles to merchandise them online.

Dale's interest in computers and technology led to a conversation with Digital MotorWorks and the creation of the automotive industry's first platform that managed the transfer of vehicle data between original equipment manufacturers, deal-erships, and third-party classified sites.

Dale joined Digital MotorWorks and eventually led its sale to ADP.

The second entrepreneurial opportunity arrived after Dale had been asked to leave ADP and found himself unemployed.

At the time, Dale knew that dealers were struggling to adapt to the rise of internet-driven used vehicle market effi-ciency and price transparency. Dale also understood that the presence of more and more vehicles and prices online, while disruptive, created an unprecedented source of market supply and demand information.

Dale created and launched vAuto and the Velocity Method of Management to help dealers attune their used vehicle oper-ations to the supply, demand, and pricing dynamics of their local markets.

By 2010, vAuto had gained critical mass. That year, Dale and the vAuto leadership team sold the company to Cox Automotive.

Today, Dale serves as executive vice president for Cox Automotive and continues to shape vAuto's strategic planning and development.

Throughout his career and life, Dale has been an avid reader. He always has at least one book underway, and another waiting on the bedside table.

During the early work with vAuto and Velocity, Dale real-ized that the stories he shared of dealers adopting Velocity and seeing success had the greatest impact with dealers who were unfamiliar with Velocity principles.

The realization led to a best-selling, three-book series on Velocity adoption and principles.

In 2017, Dale published *Like I See It*, a book that aims to help dealers prepare for a different retail environment as technology disrupts traditional vehicle ownership, purchase practices, and transportation choices.

With *Gross Deception*, Dale returns to the writing bench to disclose how the used vehicle market has changed yet again, and to help dealers adapt to these changes by deploying an investment value–based methodology for managing their used vehicle departments.

Dale received his B.S. in business administration from Indiana University and is a graduate of the General Motors Institute of Automotive Development. He also earned a law degree from DePaul University's College of Law and is a four-time winner of the American Jurisprudence Award for top performance in his class.

In addition to sharing his sought-after perspective at industry and dealer group events, Dale writes regularly at www.dalepollak.com.